The **AA POCKET**Guide
BARBADOS

Barbados: Regions and Best places to see

Original text by Lee Karen Stow

Updated by Sue Bryant

© Automobile Association Developments Limited 2008. First published 2008

ISBN: 978-0-7495-5747-8

Published by AA Publishing, a trading name of Automobile Association Developments Limited, whose registered office is Fanum House, Basing View, Basingstoke, Hampshire RG21 4EA. Registered number 1878835.

Colour separation: Keenes, Andover
Printed and bound in Italy by Printer Trento S.r.l.
Front cover images: (t) AA/Peter Baker; (b) AA/Lee Karen Stow
Back cover image: AA/James Jims

A03604
Maps in this title produced from:
    map data supplied by Global Mapping, Brackley, UK © 2007
    map data © Borch GmbH
    map data from Mountain High Maps® Copyright © 1993 Digital Wisdom, Inc

About this book

This book is divided into four sections.

Planning pages 18–31
Before you go; Getting there; Getting around; Being there

Best places to see pages 32–53
The unmissable highlights of any visit to Barbados

Exploring pages 54–115
The best places to visit in Barbados, organized by area

Maps pages 119–128
All map references are to the atlas section. For example, Bathsheba has the reference ✚ 121 E6 – indicating the page number and grid square in which it can be found

Contents

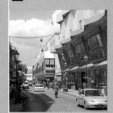

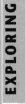

INDEX & ACKNOWLEDGEMENTS

MAPS

Planning

Before you go

WHEN TO GO

JAN	FEB	MAR	APR	MAY	JUN	JUL	AUG	SEP	OCT	NOV	DEC
27°C	27°C	27°C	27°C	27°C	27°C	31°C	31°C	27°C	27°C	27°C	27°C
81°F	81°F	81°F	81°F	81°F	81°F	88°F	88°F	81°F	81°F	81°F	81°F

High season Low season

Barbados enjoys a tropical climate with an average daytime high of 75–85°F (24–29°C) and slightly cooler nights. The rainy season is from June to November, with short, sharp showers most afternoons, followed by warm sunshine again. If hurricanes are going to develop, they usually do so between June and October, but Barbados tends to be outside their path as the island is a long way east and separate from the main Caribbean chain of landmasses. The last direct hit was in 1955.

WHAT YOU NEED

● Required
○ Suggested
▲ Not required

Some countries require a passport to remain valid for a minimum period (usually at least six months) beyond the date of entry – contact their consulate or embassy or your travel agency for details.

	UK	Germany	USA	Netherlands	Spain
Passport valid for 6 months beyond date of departure/national ID card	●	●	●	●	●
Visa (regulations can change – check before booking your trip)	▲	▲	▲	▲	▲
Onward or return ticket	●	●	●	●	●
Health inoculations (polio, tetanus, typhoid, hepatitis A)	○	○	○	○	○
Health documentation (▶ 21, Health Insurance)	○	○	○	○	○
Travel insurance	○	○	○	○	○
Driving license (current or international)	●	●	●	●	●
Car insurance certificate (if own car)	○	○	○	○	○
Car registration document (if own car)	▲	▲	▲	▲	▲

WEBSITES

For more information visit: www.barbados.org which is maintained by the Barbados Tourism Authority. Another useful site with general information is: www.visitbarbados.org

TOURIST OFFICES AT HOME

In the UK
Barbados Tourism Authority
263 Tottenham Court Road
London
W1T 7LA
☎ 020 7636 9448

In the USA
Barbados Tourism Authority
800 Second Avenue
2nd Floor
New York
NY 10017
☎ 212 986 6516
Toll Free 1 800 221 9831

HEALTH INSURANCE

If you fall ill, hotels can arrange a doctor to come and see you. If things get serious, the hospital is never far away on this small island. Full medical insurance is highly recommended and should cover you for medical and hospital costs, transportation to a suitable off-island medical facility if required, repatriation and permanent disability. Note that you will need additional coverage for certain sports such as scuba diving.

TIME DIFFERENCES

| GMT | Barbados | Germany | USA (NY) | Netherlands | Spain |
| 12 noon | 8AM | 1PM | 7AM | 1PM | 1PM |

Barbados is four hours behind the UK, five hours in British Summer Time. The island is one hour ahead of East Coast Time. Time does, however, take on different meaning in the Caribbean and visitors should expect to slow their pace accordingly.

NATIONAL HOLIDAYS

January 1 *New Year's Day*
January 22 *Errol Barrow Day*
March or April *Easter*
April 28 *National Heroes Day*

May 1 *Labor Day*
Last Monday in May *Whit Monday*
August 1 *Emancipation Day*
August 6 *Kadooment Day*

November 30 *Independence Day*
December 25 *Christmas Day*
December 26 *Boxing Day*

WHAT'S ON WHEN

December–May Polo season, with fixtures throughout at the island's four fields.

January *Barbados Jazz Festival* One week of live jazz from top artistes like Macy Gray and Anita Baker. At Sunbury Plantation House and Farley Hill.

February *Holetown Festival* A week-long celebration of the first settlement of the island, brought to life with fashion shows, sporting events and parades.

February/March *Gold Cup Festival, Garrison Savannah* The year's most glamorous and prestigious horse race.

March *Holders Season* Two weeks of music, opera and theater at Holders House, St James. A glamorous society event that attracts visitors from all over the world.

April *Fish Festival* A celebration of the fruits of the sea, with dancing, music and a lot of fish at Oistins, the epicenter of the island's fishing industry.

May *Gospelfest*, attracting singers and choirs from all over the Caribbean. *Bridgetown Film Festival*.

July/August *Crop Over* The year's biggest event, traditionally celebrating a successful sugar cane harvest. Five weeks of parades, live bands, calypso music and exhibitions, culminating in the lavish Grand Kadooment carnival parade.

Getting there

BY AIR

Grantley Adams International Airport

N/A

40 minutes

30 minutes

9 miles (15km) to city centre

Barbados is served by, among others, American Airlines, BWIA, Air Jamaica, US Airways, Air Canada, British Airways, Virgin Atlantic, Caribbean Star and LIAT. Visitors arrive at Grantley Adams International Airport in the south. It is the island's only airport and has recently been refurbished. Now, there are shops, exchange facilities and restaurants. British Airways and BWIA offer first- and business-class lounges. Departing passengers pay a tax of US$12.50 or Bds$25.
Airport and flight information ☎ 428 7101; www.gaia.com.bb

BY SEA

Cruise passengers dock at the Deep Water harbor in Bridgetown, at the stylish Cruise Passenger Terminal with duty-free (tax-free) shopping, banking and other facilities.

Getting around

PUBLIC TRANSPORT

Internal flights There are no internal flights within Barbados. Air LIAT, BWIA, American Eagle, Tropicair, Trans Island Air, Air Martinique and Caribe Express operate flights to neighboring islands in the Caribbean.

Helicopters can be chartered for either private transport or "flightseeing" from Bajan Helicopters at the Bridgetown Heliport ☎ 431 0069; www.bajanhelicopters.com

Trains There are no rail services on Barbados.

Buses Buses are an excellent, inexpensive way of getting around. Frequent services run to most parts of the island and all services terminate in Speightstown. A flat fare of Bds$1.50 takes you anywhere. There are two main types of bus: government-owned (blue with a yellow stripe) for which you must have the correct fare, and privately owned mini buses (yellow with a blue stripe) which give change. Destinations are clearly marked on the front or painted on the sides. From Bridgetown, buses run from terminals on Fairchild Street for the south and from Lower Green to the west coast and north. In addition to the main buses there are also the privately owned ZRs, these mini buses, which are white with a maroon stripe, leave from Probyn Street, River Road and Cheapside terminals. For general enquiries ☎ 436 6820.

Boat trips Organized tours of the coastline are available, plus trips to neighboring Caribbean islands.

EXCURSIONS

Numerous companies offer tours of the island; some of them, like Island Safari, in four-wheel drive vehicles, take visitors off-road through the sugar cane fields and along the east coast to beautiful and remote beach spots.

If you book a tour, many of the tour companies will pick you up from your hotel. If this is how you plan to see the island, you may not need a car for the entire duration of your stay.

WALKING

The Barbados National Trust organizes regular hikes for three levels of ability, in the morning, afternoon or moonlight. This is a great way to see the island and meet local people. The hikes are free, although donations to the Trust are welcome. For a calendar, visit www.barbados.org/hike1.htm

FARES AND TICKETS

Visitors booking through a tour operator should ask about the Barbados VIP Card, valid from May to November (excluding the Crop Over festival period in July) and offering "Buy one, get one free" deals at most of the main attractions and several restaurants.

Many attractions have two levels of pricing, one for locals and one for visitors. This may seem unfair but it reflects the much lower incomes that local Bajans receive, and the fact that the government encourages locals to make the most of their island.

TAXIS

Cabs may be expensive but they can make sense if there
are a number of you who want to travel around. Identified
by ZR number plates or painted white with a maroon stripe,
the cabs are clean, efficient and many have air conditioning.
There are no meters, but fares are regulated by the
government and published by the tourist office in
Bridgetown. Expect to pay around Bds$30 from the airport
to the south coast, or Bds$75 from the airport to
Speightstown. Taxis can be hired for private tours, too, at
about US$25 per hour. This is often worthwhile as the
drivers are very knowledgeable and are full of gossip and local lore.

DRIVING

- Speed limit on highways: 50mph/80kph
- Speed limit on main roads: 30mph/50kph (inner city 25mph/40kph)
- Speed limit on minor roads: 30mph/50kph (inner city 25mph/40kph)
- Seat belts must be worn at all times and in rear seats where fitted.
- Although there are no specific limits on drinking and driving, you should
  always drive with due care and attention. You may find that your
  insurance cover is not valid for accidents due to alcohol.
- Fuel is available in leaded, unleaded, premium and diesel. Bridgetown
  has one 24-hour fuel station. Others around the island have varying
  opening and closing times. Most close on Sundays, so you are advised
  to fill up before you travel at weekends.
- In the event of a breakdown contact your rental agency, which will
  either send help or replace the vehicle.

CAR RENTAL

Choose anything from a Mini Moke to an air-conditioned sedan. Rent on
arrival at the airport or from your hotel. Vehicles can be hired for an hour,
day, week or longer on production of a current driving license and a major
credit card. You must buy a driving permit for Bds$10, issued from the car
rental companies or the Ministry of Transport ☎ 427 2623. To rent a car,
you must be over 21 and under 75. Bicycles and mopeds are also available
for rent.

Being there

TOURIST OFFICES

The head office of the Barbados
Tourism Authority is on Harbour
Road, Bridgetown and there are
booths at the airport and the
cruise terminal.

MONEY

Barbados's currency is the Barbados dollar (Bds$) which is fixed against
the US dollar (Bds$2=US$1) and divided into 100 cents. Both US and
Barbados dollars are accepted, and major credit cards can be used at
most hotels, restaurants and stores. International banks include Barclays
Bank plc and Canadian Imperial Bank of Commerce. At Grantley Adams
International Airport, the Barbados Bank is open daily from 8am until the
last flight departs.

TIPS/GRATUITIES

Yes ✓   No ✗

Restaurants (10–15% service usually included)	✗	
Cafés/bars (10% service included)	✗	
Tour guides	✓	US$10
Taxis	✓	10% of the fare
Chambermaids	✓	US$2 per room per day
Cloakroom attendants	✓	US$4
Toilets	✓	change
Porters	✓	US$1 per bag

POSTAL SERVICES

Postal services are good. The main Post Office is in Cheapside,
Bridgetown ☎ 427 5772, open Monday to Friday 8–5. Each parish has its
own smaller post office, usually open 7:30am–12 noon and 1pm–3pm,
and stamps are available from most hotels and book stores as well as the
airport and the cruise terminal. Mail boxes are red.

TELEPHONES

Satellite links and direct dialing are available. All local calls are free except from pay phones where 25 cent coins are needed. Barbados has 95 percent coverage from the Digicel cellular network as well as a couple of other cellular providers. Phones set up for GSM 900, 1800 or 1900 will work on the island. Check roaming costs with your provider at home before traveling.

International dialing codes
From Barbados to:
UK 0 11 44
Germany 0 11 49
USA and Canada 0 11 1
Netherlands 00 11 31

Emergency telephone numbers
Police 211
Fire 311
Ambulance 511 or 911

EMBASSIES AND CONSULATES
UK ☎ 430 7800
Germany ☎ 427 1876
Netherlands ☎ 418 8074
USA ☎ 436 4950

HEALTH ADVICE
Sun advice The Caribbean sun is extremely strong and you must protect your skin. Choose a good-quality, high sun protection factor sunscreen and reapply frequently, especially after swimming and water sports. Avoid the midday sun. Wear good sunglasses and if possible, a wide-brimmed hat. Limit your time in the sun when first going to the beach. If you do suffer sunburn, stay out of the sun until you recover. Beach vendors sell aloe vera, which is very soothing for sunburn. If headache, nausea or dizziness occur, call a doctor.

Drugs Prescriptions and non-prescription drugs and medicines are available from pharmacies.

Safe water Barbados water is very pure, having been filtered by the island's natural coral. It can be enjoyed straight from the tap.

PERSONAL SAFETY

You may be approached and asked to buy marijuana or harder drugs. Politely refuse and walk away. Keep a close eye on belongings and if possible, leave valuables in the hotel safe or room safe. Don't walk the beaches at night and avoid unfamiliar neighborhoods. Don't leave valuables in cars.

ELECTRICITY

The power supply in Barbados is 110 volts 50 cycles. Carry an adapter to make sure your appliances fit the two-prong sockets. Many hotels can also supply adapters.

OPENING HOURS

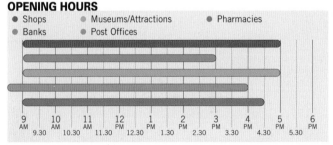

● Shops ● Museums/Attractions ● Pharmacies
● Banks ● Post Offices

9 AM | 9.30 | 10 AM | 10.30 | 11 AM | 11.30 | 12 PM | 12.30 | 1 PM | 1.30 | 2 PM | 2.30 | 3 PM | 3.30 | 4 PM | 4.30 | 5 PM | 5.30 | 6 PM

Some stores are also open on Saturday mornings 9–1. Museums are open slightly later in high season. Banks are open 9–5 on Fridays. Pharmacies are also open on Saturdays 8–1. Some do open 24 hours but not all. Check first by phoning a division of the tourist office ☎ 427 2623. There is a clinic on 3rd Avenue Bellivill, on the outskirts of Bridgetown, St Michael, which is open until midnight ☎ 228 6120. Other pharmacies include Grants on Fairchild Street, Bridgetown ☎ 436 6120 and in Oistins ☎ 428 9481; and Knights on Lower Broad Street, Bridgetown ☎ 426 5196.

LANGUAGE

Barbados experienced 300 years of British rule and as a result, the official language of the island is English. Everyone speaks and understands English so there is no need to learn the strong and lively West Indian dialect spoken by the local Barbadians (or Bajans as they are also known), and wrongly assumed to be nothing more than broken English. To try to imitate Bajan speak could actually sound false and inappropriate, so it's best to talk normally. Likewise, listening to rapid Bajan speak can be confusing. If you cannot grasp the essence of the conversation, simply ask the speaker to slow down and you'll soon pick up the essential points. Listening to two Bajans in conversation is fascinating, the sound melodic with a distinct laid-back rhythm.

Visitors who insist on learning a few Bajan words however, can buy Learn to Speak Bajan booklets from some souvenir and book stores. The dialect is not difficult to learn. Words such as "three" become "tree," the common "the" is shortened to "de," "them" becomes "dem" and "your" is a spirited "yo" or "yuh." Sometimes the response to a question is a

beautifully rich "doan' know child." Whatever language you speak, though, remember always to remain polite. In Barbados, it is common etiquette to say please, thank you and greet people with a cheerful good morning/afternoon/evening.

Bajan is a dialect which sounds, although it isn't, like broken English. It is a rich, beautiful language all of its own.

Noticeably common is the replacement of "th" with "de," as in:

wid	–	with
den	–	then
dey	–	they
de	–	the
dere	–	there
dese	–	these

Verbs have no participle endings such as -ed, so a Bajan would say "he fish' instead of "he fished," or "she cook" instead of "she cooked."

Also, the present time is spoken as a real, ongoing thing, for example: "the woman dances to the beat of the steel drum" would be "de woman she dancing to de beat o'de drum." Here are a few wonderful gems to make your ears twitch:

agen	–	again
evaht'ing	–	everything
evaht'ing cook and curry	–	everything's all taken care of
dat ol talk	–	idle gossip
a pot o'Bajan soup	–	a dish of stew
boil up	–	bring to the boil
cook up	–	all ingredients are cooked together
limin	–	hanging around
piece o'pumpkin		
and piece o'pigtail	–	ingredients for the pot
if greedy wait, hot will cool	–	wait until the dish cools and you can eat
the sea en' got no back door	–	if you get into a mess, you might not get out of it
big bout yah	–	you got fame/money/looks/talent

Best places to see

1 Andromeda Botanic Gardens

A profusion of both indigenous and tropical plants and flowers pays tribute to the mythical Greek princess Andromeda in this garden by the ocean.

Bathsheba (➤ 38), on the rugged eastern coastline, makes a dramatic setting for this garden established in 1954 by the late amateur horticulturist Mrs Iris Bannochie. Mrs Bannochie devoted herself to the garden, creating trails of blossoms and tropical foliage on the cliffs above the Atlantic, and collected many rare species of plant on her trips around the world. She named her creation after Andromeda (daughter of King Cepheus of Ethiopia) who, according to legend, was chained at the water's edge as a sacrifice to the sea monster before being rescued by Perseus.

Cascading streams and waterfalls have been added, and the gardens are building up a collection of medicinal plants with information on their traditional uses. Andromeda is astonishingly beautiful, awash with frangipani *(Plumeria rubra),* bougainvillaea *(Bougainvillaea spectabilis),* traveler's trees *(Ravenala madagascariensis)* and orchids *(Orchidaceae).* Through strategically scattered palms you

glimpse the azure blue of the ocean from viewpoints on the pathways. The fishing village in the distance is Tent Bay. As you admire Andromeda, Barbados monkeys swing in the trees above, and there are mongooses and lizards.

In 1988, before her death, Iris Bannochie donated her gardens to the Barbados National Trust. The Trust now offers tours led by knowledgeable volunteer horticulturists on Wednesdays at 10:30am. If you prefer to go it alone, there's a choice of two self-guided trails, one covering hilly areas and taking up to an hour, and the other a half-hour, easier stroll.

✚ 121 E6 ✉ Bathsheba, St Joseph ☎ 433 9261 or 433 9384 ◷ Daily 9–5 (except public holidays) 🖐 Moderate 🍴 Light meals and afternoon tea served at the Hibiscus Café ($$). The cook will also prepare a picnic lunch for you to eat in the gardens 🚌 From Bridgetown, Speightstown ❓ Further information from the Barbados National Trust (☎ 426 2421, http://trust.funbarbados.com)

2 Barbados Wildlife Reserve

www.barbadosmonkey.org

This natural mahogany forest, home to exotic animals, birds and reptiles, also features buildings made of coral stone and relics of the sugar industry.

While sipping a cold drink at the mahogany bar here, don't be surprised to see a red-footed Barbados tortoise stroll by. Except for caged parrots and a python, the animals here mostly roam freely over the 4 acres (1.5ha) of forest. The reserve is built from coral stone gathered from surrounding canefields and its paths are made of bricks (still carrying the manufacturer's stamp) from 17th- and 18th-century sugar factories.

Children love it here, but they must be supervised as some of the animals, including the monkeys, can bite. Among the mix are cattle egrets, spectacled caimans, guinea fowl, deer, pelicans, congas, flamingos, cockatoos, toucans and peacocks. In a straw-carpeted pen, iguanas of the West Indies, the largest vertebrates native to the Caribbean islands, sprawl on logs. They bake in the sun, oblivious to the rabbits hopping

around them and the juvenile tortoises crawling by. Many creatures arrived here as gifts to the reserve. The agoutis and the armadillos are from the forestry departments in St Lucia and St Vincent, while the pelicans hail from Florida.

To see the Barbados green (or vervet) monkeys, be here between 2–3pm, when the colony returns from the forests of Grenade Hall (➤ 84). Originally introduced from West Africa, the monkeys number around 5,000–7,000 on the island and just one animal can provide up to 2.5 million doses of polio vaccine. The reserve's Primate Research Center, focusing on the use and conservation of the monkey, is responsible for up to 70 percent of the world's production of the vaccine.

✚ 120 C3 ✉ Farley Hill, St Peter ☎ 422 8826 🔾 Daily 10–5 (last admission 3:45) 🖐 Moderate, children half price. Includes admission to Grenade Hall Forest and Signal Station 🍴 Café ($) 🚌 Continuous bus service from Bridgetown, Holetown, Speightstown and Bathsheba ❓ Several sightseeing operators visit the reserve

3 Bathsheba

This tiny beauty spot on the east coast has a great appeal for those wanting to see the rugged, natural face of Barbados.

There are no luxury hotels at Bathsheba and you won't find anyone to park your car. Even in peak season, this fishing village is devoid of crowds. Its coves and bays are washed by excellent surf and surfing champions ride the waves from September to December at the frothy Soup Bowl at the center of the beach. Two rows of giant, grass-covered boulders seem to guard the bay from the threat of the approaching tide. In fact, apart from the bathing pools that fill up and can be enjoyed at low tide, it's far too dangerous to swim here.

What you can do, though, is stroll by the church and the pastel-painted houses or wander along the deserted beaches backed by chalky cliffs and wild hills. There are no formal attractions here, just the peace and scenery. Nearby are the green hills of Cattlewash, so-called because the cattle wander down to the ocean to take a bath.

In Victorian times, Bathsheba was a magnet for vacationing

Barbadians who would come to take the air. A railroad ran from Bridgetown to Bathsheba from 1883 until it closed in 1937. Its life was precarious, suffering from landslides, underfunding and mismanagement. Coastal erosion was so bad the crew often had to get out to repair the track.

✚ 121 E6 🍴 New Edgewater Hotel ($) – for the Sunday Bajan buffet, 12–3, book in advance 🚌 Continuous bus service from Bridgetown, Holetown and Speightstown

4 Chalky Mount Village

www.highland-pottery.com

You can watch pottery being made and fired traditionally and enjoy fabulous views of the Scotland District in the chalk hills of St Andrew.

The skilled potter Winston Junior Paul and his wife, Prim, run Highland Pottery, a uniquely placed workshop high in Chalky Mount Village. It stands on a geological formation said to resemble a sleeping man with his hands folded over his stomach. Locals refer to it as "Napoleon". At one time over 20 pottery businesses thrived here, the studios and workshops humming in wood houses high on the hills. Today, only a couple struggle to make a living, battling against cheap imports. Beneath them is the brown-red clay dug to create the artists' pieces. Winston's workshop is like a tree house, open on all sides to let in the

refreshing breezes. It has a 360-degree view of
the undulating eastern landscape, known as the
Scotland District, that rambles down to the Atlantic.

Winston tells you how the clay is first mixed
with water then sieved to take out the tree roots.
The mixture is then laid out on drying trays in the
sun for about three weeks until the water has
evaporated. Next it is brought indoors where the
rushing wind dries out the last of the water. He
invites you to watch him knead the clay on the
wedging table, squeezing out the bubbles before
slapping it down on the potter's wheel. Before the
advent of electricity, pots were thrown on a kick
wheel, which is made of cement and shaped like a
millstone. The wheel is kicked to rotate the clay and
Winston is so skilled at it that he appears to be
running while shaping a flower vase before your
eyes. He then fires the pots in the kiln, after which
they are painted and
glazed and displayed
on shelves.

➕ 121 D5 ✉ Chalky Mount
Potteries, Chalky Mount,
Scotland District ☎ 431 0747
🕐 Daily 9–5 💷 Free
🍽 Restaurants/cafés ($–$$)
at Bathsheba 🚌 From
Bridgetown

5 Flower Forest and Orchid World

This colorful duo, featuring tropical and native trees and spectacular orchids, lies on a popular scenic route in the parishes of St Joseph and St John.

Flower Forest

Set 846ft (258m) above sea level on a former sugar plantation, the 50-acre (20ha) forest has a visitor center furnished with old copper sugar-boiling vats and decorated with a mural depicting the plantation's history. From here a nature trail leads through a tropical corridor of neatly labeled plants and trees. Look for the native bearded fig tree *(Ficus citrifolia),* bamboos and breadfruit *(Artocarpus altilis),* plus the Queen of Flowers tree, which was planted by Princess Alexandra in 1992. Some rest spots overlook manicured lawns, the most splendid being Liv's Lookout, with views of the rugged Scotland District and the island's highest point, Mount Hillaby, at 1,115ft (340m).

Orchid World

Opened by Prime Minister Owen Arthur in 1998, Orchid World lies in the high rainfall area of the island, which averages 79in (203cm) annually. Rainwater is collected in a 29,920-gal (136,000 liter) tank and, as much as possible, recycled. This

makes for a healthy environment for a plethora of orchid species that is continually being added to. Orchids spring up everywhere, and *vandas*, *schomburgkia* and *oncidium* grow by the paths. *Epiphytes*, or air plants, dangle from wire frames in the specially controlled environment of the orchid houses. Coral, limestone rockeries, caves and a babbling stream add to the tranquillity of the garden, which has a far-reaching view across the silvery sheen of the sugar cane fields.

Flower Forest

✚ 120 E4 ✉ Richmond, St Joseph ☎ 433 8152 ⏰ Daily 9–5 (last tour 4pm) 🖐 Moderate 🍴 On site café ($) 🚌 From Bridgetown take the Chalky Mount or Sugar Hill bus and ask the driver to drop you off near the forest

Orchid World

✚ 124 B2 ✉ Between Gun Hill and St John's Church, Highway 3b ☎ 433 0306 ⏰ Daily 9–5 (last admission 4:30) 🖐 Moderate 🍴 Café ($) 🚌 From Bridgetown take the Sargeant Street bus

6 Garrison Historic Area

Once the defense nucleus of Barbados, the Garrison consists of a circle of mid-17th century military buildings and an exceptional cannon collection.

When Oliver Cromwell took control of England after the Civil War of 1648, he set his sights on Barbados. But Lord Willoughby, the governor of Barbados, decided to strengthen the island's defense. Needham's Fort, later renamed Charles Fort, today

stands as the oldest building, dating back to 1650. It was strengthened by the addition of another fort, St Ann's, now the headquarters of the Barbados Defense Force.

When France declared war on Britain in 1778, an influx of British troops arrived at the Garrison. The bewildered Barbados government, which had trouble finding enough accommodations for them, were forced to build temporary barracks. The majority of troops left when the war ended.

A permanent garrison building was built to accommodate the soldiers who stayed and to prevent future attacks on the British islands. Over the years the Garrison has seen alterations but the distinctive redbrick clock tower of

the Main Guard has changed little. The 30 or so 17th- to 18th-century cannons, perhaps the world's largest collection, are housed in the Barbados Defense Force Compound at St Ann's Fort.

Since the withdrawal of the British troops from Barbados in 1905–1906, some buildings have been refurbished. The latest to receive attention is Bush Hill House where the United States' first president, George Washington, stayed in 1751. The house is now known as George Washington House and is open to the public (➤ 68). St Ann's Fort and the Main Guard are also being restored.

Horse racing takes place on the Garrison Savannah, the former parade ground. By day cricket teams practise their batting and fielding, while locals jog around the track. It was here, on November 20, 1966, that the British Union Flag was lowered and Barbados's blue and gold flag – bearing a trident – raised to mark Independence Day.

🞤 122 E3 🖂 St Michael 🖐 Free 🍴 Brown Sugar ($$)
🚌 From Bridgetown and the south coast ❓ 1.5-hour tours of the Garrison area. Own transport needed ☎ 427 1436

7 Harrison's Cave

www.harrisonscave.com

A ride on an electric tram takes you through the subterranean stream passages of a natural limestone wonder – the island's most famous site.

A labyrinth of creamy white stalagmites and stalactites dripping with rainwater, Harrison's Cave is a world away from the tropical jungle above it. Deep below the island's geographical center, you don a hard hat and hop aboard a trolley car for a 1-mile (1.5-km) long guided tour. Following a smooth underground passageway, you halt to photograph the "cathedral" chamber, a waterfall pouring into an 8-ft (2.5-m) deep pool. Nearby is a group of conical shapes known as "people's village". Alongside runs the original subterranean stream. Above hangs the "chandelier", continuously dripping with calcite-laden water. The stalactites and stalagmites have been growing over thousands of years and in some places have joined together to form pillars.

Although named after Thomas Harris who owned most of the land in the area during the early 1700s, the caves were actually discovered in 1796

by Dr George Pinckard, an English doctor who lived on the island. Several expeditions were attempted during the 18th and 19th centuries but with little success and it was not until the 1970s that the true extent of this natural wonder was revealed by a Danish speleologist and Barbadian cavers. Government-backed explorations and excavations followed and an underground stream was diverted as work on creating an attraction began.

The first tourists arrived in 1981 and the cave has since welcomed Queen Elizabeth II and musicians Paul McCartney and Elton John. The full story of the caves and how they were discovered is explained in an audiovisual show in a special theater, shown before the tour gets underway.

The cave is one of the island's "must see" sights. The surrounding facilities were completely refurbished for the 2007 Cricket World Cup and there's a new Interpretation Center, restaurant and souvenir shop.

➕ 120 F4 ✉ Welchman Hall, St Thomas
☎ 438 6640 ⏱ Tours daily at half-hourly intervals. First tour 9am, last tour 4pm
✋ Moderate 🍴 Snack bar ($–$$) on site
🚌 Bus from Bridgetown signposted Shorey Village

8 National Heroes Square, Bridgetown

Originally planned to represent London's Trafalgar Square in miniature, the capital's focal point is becoming increasingly Barbadian.

Before April 28, 1999, this main square was known as Trafalgar Square, a throwback to the days when Barbados was known as Little England. The square was renamed by the prime minister, Owen Arthur, in a ceremony that took place to mark the occasion of the second National Heroes Day. It is a holiday

that remembers notable figures in the island's history. Taxi drivers and locals, however, still call it Trafalgar Square.

During the ceremony, 10 people were honored, including Errol Walton Barrow, the first prime minister elected after independence in 1966; Bussa, the slave leader of the 1816 rebellion; cricket star Sir Garfield Sobers; and Samuel Jackman Prescod. Prescod, the son of a slave mother, rose in 1843 to become the country's first non-white member of Parliament in more than 200 years. He fought for the rights of all classes and colors.

A bronze statue of Lord Nelson was erected in the square in 1813. Nelson sailed to the island in 1805 with a large fleet, which included the *Victory*, months before he perished at the Battle of Trafalgar. For decades there has been talk of moving Nelson (he's considered as a defender of the slave trade) elsewhere and erecting a Barbadian figure, possibly that of Barrow, instead.

Opposite the admiral towers is the obelisk honoring the Barbadians killed in World Wars I and II. In the center, the Dolphin Fountain commemorates the first running water piped to the town. Surrounding the square are the neo-Gothic buildings of the seat of Parliament, including the Treasury and House of Assembly (➤ 60). This is an ideal starting point for your own walking tour of the capital.

➕ 127 D5 ✉ Junction of Broad Street and St Michael's Row, Bridgetown, St Michael ✋ Free 🍴 Numerous cafés and restaurants ($–$$) on Broad Street and along the Careenage 🚌 All buses run to Bridgetown

9 Speightstown

Brightly colored fishing boats, wooden houses and a quaint church make up this typical West Indian settlement, Barbados's second biggest town.

Speightstown (pronounced "Spitestown") might appear sleepy, but the calm is broken when the fishing boats come in and locals arrive to shop. It bears a history as a thriving port for sugar and the old commercial part is gradually being restored by the Barbados National Trust. The beautiful Arlington House, one of the National Trust's properties, is due to open to the public as an interpretive center in 2008 with the theme "Trading Memories". There's also a smart new marina, Port St Charles, now home to several gleaming yachts.

The town offers modern shopping in the Mall, bakeries serving Bajan bread, and market stalls of fruit and vegetables. There's also the chance to while away the hours in a rum shop with the Bajans on a Saturday afternoon, listening to cricket on the radio.

Founded by William Speight, Speightstown was the principal export destination for the island's sugar. Because of the town's importance, military forts were built around it for protection but today little remains of this defensive ring.

St Peter's Parish Church, one of the earliest churches on the island, dates from around 1630. Inside, the wooden gallery above was once occupied by the "poor whites", the name given to descendants of English, Irish and Scots who were imported as indentured labor to work on the sugar cane plantations.

A "Round de Town" stroll and the longer, more challenging award-winning Arbib Nature and Heritage Trail (➤ 94) organized by the Barbados National Trust both begin by the painted blue benches at the harborside, just past the Fisherman's pub.

✚ 120 D2 ✉ Speightstown, St Peter 🚌 Buses from all over the island ❓ A 2-hour "Round de Town" stroll runs on Wed, Thu and Sat from 9am or 2:30pm, depending on numbers (☎ 426 2421 🖐 Moderate)

10 Sunbury Plantation House

Bordered by gardens, this 340-year-old plantation house is crammed to the ceiling with relics from the days of the great white sugar planters.

For the best insight into how the wealthy white planters lorded it up while their slaves and laborers sweated, step inside Sunbury Plantation House. You're immediately surrounded by trappings of the rich, an outstanding collection of Victorian and Edwardian pottery, silverware and china. Anywhere else such a trove would be roped off or protected behind glass show cabinets. At Sunbury, where all the rooms are accessible, you walk among the Barbados mahogany tables and antiques as though you're waiting for the owner to return.

Originally thought to be called Chapmans after one of the first planter families, Sunbury is now owned by Mr and Mrs Keith Melville. They opened the house to the public in 1983. Highlights include the sunroom, furnished with a white rattan suite, where the ladies would mingle. Men conducted business in the office, the only room to contain the house's original curios, including a 1905 calculator. Portraits of wealthy landowners hang alongside drawings of scenes from the West Indies during the days of slavery. Upstairs, the airy bedrooms are a treat. Check out the 1920s swimming costume, the marble hip bath and the lady's silver brush set on the dressing table.

➕ 125 D5 ✉ St Philip ☎ 423 6270 🕐 Daily 9:30–4:30
✋ Moderate 🍴 Courtyard restaurant and bar ($–$$)
🚌 From Oistins to College Savannah or Bayfield
❓ A planter's candlelit dinner at Sunbury includes a five-course meal, cocktails, all drinks and a tour of the house. Reservations required. Minimum number of 10

Exploring

Bridgetown

Bridgetown

The town was originally known as Indian River Bridge, after the discovery of an Amerindian bridge that spanned the Constitution River here. Founded by British settlers in 1628, it grew up to become the island's administrative and commercial capital and principal port. Before independence in 1966 Bridgetown bowed under British sovereignty, which is why you'll detect traces of English character in its colonial architecture. Bridgetown, with the sumptuously furnished houses of the sugar planters and warehouses stocked with goods from around the globe, was compared to wealthy Port Royal in Jamaica before the latter was wiped out by an earthquake.

The bulk of Barbados's 281,000 population lives in and around the capital, with an estimated 100,000 actually within the city and suburbs. The capital is the seat of the Barbados government, with the British monarch holding executive powers and represented on the island by a governor general, who in turn advises the cabinet and appoints the prime minister. Next come 21 members of the Senate and a 28-member House of Assembly, residing in the Parliament Buildings.

Most of the attractions can be seen in half a day on a walking tour starting near National Heroes Square (also known as Trafalgar Square (► 48), with the rest of the day spent shopping and trying out the cafés and restaurants. Bridgetown is also a base for day cruises, yacht charters, a trip on the Atlantis Submarine (► 114) and scenic helicopter flights. ✛ 122 D2

BRIDGETOWN SYNAGOGUE

Tucked away off Magazine Lane and worth a visit is the Jewish Synagogue. Next door is a Jewish cemetery where weathered tombs contain the remains of Jews who arrived in Bridgetown in the 17th century and set up businesses on nearby Swan Street. The synagogue dates back to 1654, but was rebuilt in the 19th century following extensive hurricane damage. Remarkably well kept by the Barbados National Trust, it is believed to be one of the oldest synagogues in the western hemisphere. Inside, gorgeous wood paneling is brightened by the light from a quartet of brass chandeliers. Members of the island's present Jewish population still use the synagogue on a regular basis.

🏛 126 C4 ⊠ Synagogue Lane, off Magazine Lane ☎ Barbados National Trust, 426 2421 🕐 Mon–Fri 9–12, 1–4 💷 Free, donations welcome 🚌 Fairchild Street

THE CAREENAGE

Alongside the Careenage – a narrow inner harbor at the mouth of the Constitution River – a wooden boardwalk accented with ornate, green-painted street lamps takes you past dozens of charter yachts and ocean-going boats advertising tours and deep-sea fishing. On the other side of the harbor are the many restored and painted houses of The Wharf. Toward the town, the boardwalk leads back to the main square or across Chamberlain Bridge to Independence Arch. Built in 1987, this monument commemorates the 21st anniversary of the island's independence.

➕ 126 E3 ✉ The Wharf, off National Heroes Square 🖐 Free 🍴 Waterfront cafés ($–$$)
🚌 Fairchild Street, main bus terminal

MONTEFIORE FOUNTAIN

The Montefiore Fountain, built in memory of a Jewish businessman called John Montefiore, was originally installed in Beckwith Place. Its position today, on what looks like a traffic island in Coleridge Street, seems inappropriate for such a beauty. Look closely and you'll see the figures of Fortitude, Temperance, Patience and Justice portrayed. The accompanying inscription reads, "Look to the end; Be sober-minded; To bear is to conquer; Do wrong to no one."

✚ 126 B4 ✉ Coleridge Street ✋ Free
🚌 Fairchild Street

NATIONAL HEROES SQUARE

Best places to see ➤ 48–49.

PARLIAMENT BUILDINGS

Though Barbados has the third oldest parliament in the whole of the Commonwealth, established in 1639 with an all-white House of Assembly, the Parliament Buildings to the north of National Heroes Square are younger. This is due to the number of fires that blighted the town, the most devastating occurring in 1766. Following the fire of 1860, the Parliament Buildings you see now were built in neo-Gothic style. This group includes the Senate and the House of Assembly, the latter fitted with stained-glass windows depicting British monarchs and Oliver Cromwell. The clock tower is not the original; that was demolished in 1884 and a new one built two years later in 1886. Here sat the decision-makers, colonists of the 1700s busily reaping the rewards of sugar cane farming. You can imagine them fretting over

whether the "mother country," England, would interfere with their right to self-government, or whether their slaves were plotting to rebel. The West Wing has been refurbished and there is talk of opening a National Heroes Gallery, but details were not available at the time of writing.

🕇 127 D5 ✉ Top of Broad Street

a walk around Bridgetown

Begin at National Heroes Square (➤ 48) and exit the square along St Michael's Row for a look in St Michael's Cathedral (➤ 65).

Continue up St Michael's Row until you reach the gates of Queen's Park (➤ 64).

Stroll through the grounds, peer into the Georgian house, and find the African baobab tree.

Head back to National Heroes Square by the same route and turn right up Marthill Street. The road veers left and then right onto Magazine Lane.

You'll soon come to Synagogue Lane on the left, which leads to the Bridgetown Synagogue (➤ 58) and, behind a low wall to the right of the building, the Jewish cemetery.

Return to Magazine Lane, turning left toward the Montefiore Fountain (➤ 60).

Behind the fountain are the law courts, library and police station. Until they were closed in 1878, the law courts housed the Town Hall Gaol. Behind is Tudor Street, one of the oldest streets in the city.

Continue southwestward along Coleridge Street, turning right onto Swan Street. At the junction (intersection) with Milk Market turn left and continue until you reach the throng of Broad Street.

Once known as New England Street, Broad Street is Bridgetown's main thoroughfare, lined with stores selling

duty-free jewelry, rums, perfumes, leather goods and other tourist goods. An eyecatcher is the sugary pink-and-white Victorian facade of Da Costa's Mall.

At this point you can either take a detour right and stroll along the boardwalk around The Careenage (▶ 59), or continue to the starting point of the walk near the Nelson statue.

Distance Approximately 1.25 miles (2km)
Time 3 hours or half a day with lunch, shopping and rest stops
Start/End Point National Heroes Square ✚ 127 D5
✉ Fairchild Street
Lunch Waterfront Café ($–$$)

QUEEN'S PARK

One of the attractions in the park is the 89ft-high (27m) baobab, estimated to be 1,000 years old and believed to have originated in Guinea, West Africa. Its circumference is 82ft (25m). In the pleasant park surrounding the baobab you'll see Barbadians in suits resting for lunch and children playing on the steps of the bandstand. The white Georgian building, Queen's Park House, was once the home of the commander of the British troops. It is now devoted to exhibitions of local arts and the theater.

➕ 127 C8 ✉ End of St Michael's Row ⏰ Daily 💷 Free
🚌 Fairchild Street

ST MICHAEL'S CATHEDRAL

The cool and tranquil cathedral, also known as the Cathedral Church of St Michael and All Angels, began as a small wooden church with enough seats for a congregation of 100 people. It was built between 1660 and 1665, but was destroyed by a hurricane in 1780 and had to be rebuilt. The new St Michael's became a cathedral when William Hart Coleridge, the first bishop of the island, arrived on Barbados in 1825.

www.stmichaelbarbados.com

✚ 127 D6 ✉ St Michael's Row ☎ 427 0790 ⏱ Daily 9–5 💷 Free, donations welcome 🚌 Fairchild Street

More to see around Bridgetown

BARBADOS MUSEUM AND HISTORICAL SOCIETY

The Barbados Museum and Historical Society provides a wonderfully old-fashioned introduction to Barbados, housing around 250,000 objects, including West Indian fine and decorative arts, pre-Columbian archaeological pieces and African objects.

Displays begin with the evolution of the planet and a showcase of coral, a major ecosystem of the island. Tools fashioned from coral by the Arawaks and Caribs are here, as are explanations of the tribes' religious beliefs. Fast-forward to the 1600s and you come to the arrival of the English colonists. From 1627 to 1640, until sugar cane flourished, tobacco and cotton were the main crops. Planters relied heavily on African slaves to develop the sugar economy and it is estimated that around 400,000 slaves were imported to Barbados between 1627 and 1807. Their skin was stamped with the initials of their white owner, using an instrument similar to the museum's silver slave-brand dated c1800. The museum explains how, after emancipation, slaves tried to make the transition to independent islanders through schooling, farming, entertainment and music.

Outside are examples of the island's architecture and a military gallery. Prints showing the days of slavery, bequeathed to the museum by shipping magnate Sir Edward Cunard, hang in a gallery also graced with shell displays. The African Gallery is now open and redesigned to link the Caribbean with its African ancestry. Of fascinating importance is a collection of rare West Indian books, plus early maps of Barbados including the earliest known map of the island, dated 1657.

www.barbmuse.org.bb

✚ 122 E3 ✉ St Ann's Garrison, St Michael ☎ 427 0201 🕐 Mon–Sat 9–5, Sun 2–6 💷 Inexpensive 🍴 Several cafés nearby 🚌 Fairchild Street, or from the south alight at Garrison Savannah ❓ Specially designed tours can be arranged. A Fine Craft Festival is held on the first Sat in Dec

GARRISON HISTORIC AREA

Best places to see ➤ 44–45.

GEORGE WASHINGTON HOUSE

After seven years of fund-raising and restoration, the house on
Bush Hill where a young George Washington spent seven weeks
in 1751 was opened to the public in January 2007. America's first
president traveled with his older half-brother, Lawrence, in search
of a more temperate climate to help the latter's tuberculosis. The
Washingtons also had connections with some of the prominent
families on the island.

The two-story Georgian-style house, perched on an escarpment
overlooking Carlisle Bay, now serves as a museum and interpretive
center and also features a genealogical center which can help
Americans trace their roots on the island. Over the centuries, the
building has also served as a private home, a base for French
prisoners, offices and part of the British military garrison.
www.georgewashingtonbarbados.org

➕ 122 E3 ✉ Bush Hill, The Garrison, St Michael ☎ 228 5461 ◷ Mon–Sat
9–4:30 ❡ Inexpensive ❚❚ Café and gift shop on site

MOUNT GAY RUM VISITOR CENTER

For the rundown on rum and a sip of the neat stuff, visit the
Mount Gay Rum Visitor Center and learn the story of what is
reputedly the home of the world's oldest rum (part of Remy-
Cointreau since 1989). This is actually the blending and bottling
factory; the distillery itself is in St Lucy, in the north of the island.
Step in to a traditional-style chattel house and learn about the
history of rum since 1703, right up to how it's aged, blended and
bottled today. If you book a special luncheon tour with one of the
sightseeing operators, or through your resort/hotel rep, then
transport, a Bajan buffet and a free miniature bottle of rum are
included. Of course, you can taste the rum in comfort at
the on-site shop. Note how the bottles line wooden shelves

behind the bar as they do in rum shops all over the island.

✚ 122 D2 ✉ Brandons, Spring Garden Highway, St Michael ☎ 425 8757
🕐 Daily 8–4:30, tours 9:30 and 3:30 ✋ Moderate 🚌 From Bridgetown, take
the Holetown bus to Brandons

PELICAN CRAFT CENTER

Between the cruise terminal and Bridgetown, this
small craft center is an interesting stop if you've
decided to walk between the two. Sitting on land
reclaimed from the sea, the center's pyramidal
roofs shelter shops selling local arts and crafts. It
also has workshops where you can watch some
of the island's finest craftspeople at work.
Metalwork, glassware, wooden crafts, pottery,
paintings and batiks come with a reasonable price tag. You can
also buy Royal Barbados Cigars made by the Caribbean Cigar
Company. There is also a restaurant, and a café serves breakfast,
lunch and drinks.

✚ 122 D2 ✉ Princess Alice Highway, Bridgetown ☎ 427 5350 🕐 Mon–Fri
10–5, Sat 9–2. Hours extend during peak holiday season ✋ Free 🍴 Cork and
Bottle Café ($)

ST PATRICK'S CATHEDRAL

The cornerstone of Roman Catholic St Patrick's Cathedral was originally laid in 1840, but because of lack of funds and too few Catholics, it wasn't consecrated until decades later, in 1899. The interior is dressed with Scottish marble, Irish crests and flags. Nearby, overlooking the Esplanade and Carlisle Bay, is a statue of social reformer and former prime minister Sir Grantley Adams. He stands outside the present government's headquarters and offices of the prime minister.

✚ 122 E3 ✉ Highway 7, St Michael ◷ Daily ✋ Free, donations welcome ▐ Several choices ($–$$) on the coastal road ▣ Take buses to Bridgetown or the south coast

TYROL COT HERITAGE VILLAGE

Just over 2.5 acres (1ha) of landscaped gardens encompass Tyrol Cot Heritage Village, said to be the birthplace of Barbadian democracy. Built in 1854, the house was home to the late Sir Grantley Adams, founder of the Barbados Labor Party, from 1929. He was the first premier of Barbados and the only prime minister of the short-lived West Indies Federation. Adams was one of the 10 national heroes named by the present prime minister, who also declared Adams's birthdate (April 28, 1898) National Heroes Day and a public holiday. Adams's son, Tom, who became prime

minister from 1976 to 1985, was born here. Restored by the Barbados National Trust, the house is built of coral stone blocks. Inside it still has the Adams's own Barbadian antique furniture. Within the

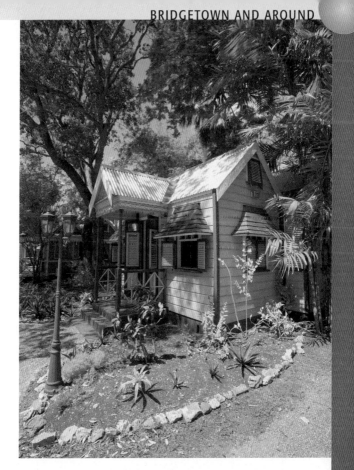

4-acre (1.5-ha) grounds is a craft village in the style of a traditional chattel house settlement – the moveable homes of plantation workers. You can buy handmade souvenirs by local artists here. There is a replica of an 1820s thatched slave hut revealing the simple way slaves lived in the days of the great sugar plantations.

✚ 122 C3 ✉ Codrington Hill, St Michael ☎ 424 2074 🕐 Mon–Fri 9–5; shops may close earlier 🔟 Inexpensive 🍴 The Rum Shop, on site 🚌 From Bridgetown, take the Cave Hill, Holders Green or Jackson bus

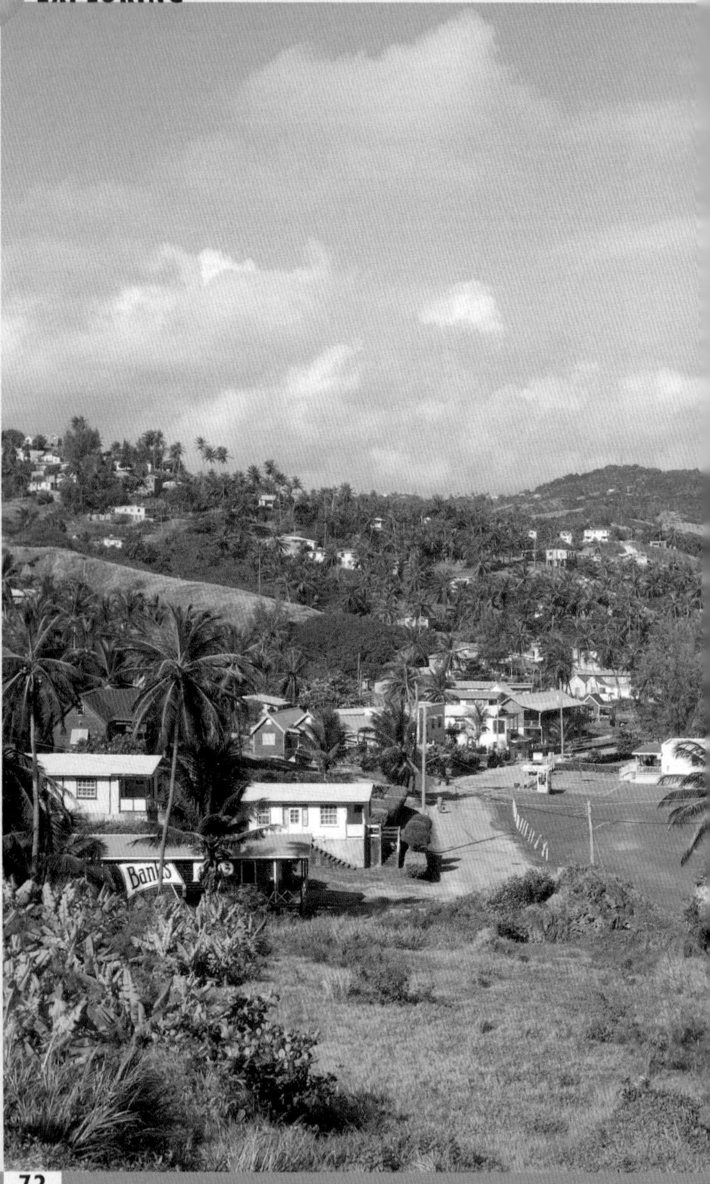
Banks

Northern Barbados

**In contrast to the south, the far
north of the island is sleepy and
undeveloped, covered with
rippling sugar cane fields sloping
down to small settlements on
sandy beaches, or in the far
north, craggy cliffs.**

Speightstown

This is where the warm
Caribbean meets the
stormy, rough Atlantic
Ocean and the scenery is
reminiscent of how Barbados
may have looked 100 years ago
before tourism developed: goats
and sheep in the fields, unassuming, often
ramshackle little houses, many churches, the occasional rum
shack and to the east, the wilder Scotland district which almost
resembles the moorlands and rolling hills after which it is named.

Holetown

ANDROMEDA BOTANIC GARDEN

Best places to see ➤ 34–35.

ANIMAL FLOWER CAVE

The cave is at North Point, unsurprisingly as far north as you can go on Barbados. When you go you can expect a breezy and exposed, yet fabulous, spot for photography. A flight of steps leads down to a cavern carved out of the coral rock where there are scattered pools containing hundreds of sea anemones. Natural historian Griffith Hughes described them as animal flowers in 1750. Look behind you and the view of the ocean is amazing. Look down and you'll see the pools are deep enough to swim in, but be careful of the slippery surface.

➕ 120 A3 ✉ St Lucy ☎ 439 8797 🕐 Daily 9:30–5 ♿ Inexpensive 🍴 Café ($) serving snacks 🚌 From Bridgetown take the Connell town bus

BATHSHEBA
Best places to see ➤ 38–39.

BARBADOS POLO CLUB
Polo on the island dates back to the 1900s and was introduced by the British cavalry who, having tired of playing against each other, roped in the locals. The Barbados Polo Club was established at what is now the historic Garrison in Bridgetown in 1929 and moved in the 1960s to its current location on Holders Hill in St James, with its wide grassland and towering trees. Recently, three new polo fields have been developed. Each year, from between October and the end of May, the season's itinerary includes fixtures against international teams, bolstered by Bajan hospitality. These matches are well attended by tourists, many of whom regard Barbados polo as one of the most vibrant sports on the island. Afternoon tea and cucumber sandwiches are served in style in the atmospheric wooden clubhouse after the game.
✚ 122 B2 ✉ Holders Hill, St James ☎ 427 0022 👆 Free, but priced tickets for international matches

BARBADOS WILDLIFE RESERVE
Best places to see ➤ 36–37.

along East Coast Road

a drive

The East Coast Road (also called the Ermie Bourne Highway) runs through the parishes of St Andrew and St Joseph between the Atlantic Ocean and the Scotland District. Opened in 1966 by Queen Elizabeth II, the road slithers along the route of the old railway from Bridgetown to Bellaplaine and passes three of our Best Places to See.

Have your hotel prepare a picnic lunch beforehand so you can stop and spend an hour sitting on the sands and watching the surfers. Remember, it is too dangerous for swimming, but at low tide you can explore the rock pools.

Start from Bathsheba (➤ 38). Spend a while at Andromeda Botanic Gardens (➤ 34) and Bathsheba village before heading north, keeping the ocean to your right.

Worn, wooden chattel houses face deserted beaches scattered with rock formations and giant boulders. Next comes Cattlewash (➤ 38). The road here is not busy, so you can stop at intervals to take photographs. The Scotland District on your left, so called because it reminded British settlers of the Scottish Highlands, is a rugged area of steep lanes with sheep and cattle grazing on the hillsides. Many potters exploit the clay deposits in this area (➤ 40).

Drive on a little farther to reach a peaceful resting spot, Barclays Park, a picnic area popular with locals on public holidays. On weekdays, you might be the only visitor. The park was a gift from Barclays Bank in 1966, the year of independence.

This short drive ends at the village of
Bellaplaine, where the railroad once
terminated.

Distance 4 miles (6.5km)
Time Half a day with lunch and stops
Start Point Bathsheba ✚ 121 E6
End Point Bellaplaine ✚ 126 E3
Lunch Take a picnic or have a buffet at New
Edgewater Hotel ($$)

❓ The drive can be done in reverse and linked with part of the drive
to the island's northern tip (➤ 86)

CHALKY MOUNT VILLAGE
Best places to see ➤ 40–41.

EARTHWORKS POTTERY
Earthworks Pottery is another showcase for Barbadian art crafted from local clay. Founded in 1983 as a small art studio making individual pieces, the pottery has expanded and now produces a range of trinket bowls, carvings and custom-made tiles – and yes – all major credit cards are accepted. It's a bright and cheerful place where practically everything except the trees and grass are

painted. There's also a batik studio and an art gallery. After touring the pottery and watching the artists, you can dine on light meals on the veranda next to a bamboo patch.

www.earthworks-pottery.com

🕇 122 B4 ✉ St Thomas ☎ 425 0223
🕐 Mon–Fri 9–5 (except public hols),
Sat 9–1 ✋ Free 🍴 Treehouse Café
($–$$) ☎ 425 0223) 🚌 From Bridge-
town, take Hillaby or Shop Hill bus

FARLEY HILL NATIONAL PARK

Once the most imposing mansion on Barbados, 19th-century Farley Hill at Farley Hill National Park was built to show off the accumulated wealth of the sugar planters. Originally known as Grenade Hall, it came into the hands of Sir Thomas Graham Briggs, who named it Farley Hill. Amid the fire-damaged ruins, overgrown with plants, you can imagine the sumptuous parties held here during the heyday of the sugar boom. Prince Alfred, the second son of Queen Victoria, and Prince George (later George V of England) arrived in carriages to take luncheon or dinner. Though you can't enter the roofless house for safety reasons, you can get a good look at the ruins through its windowless frames. It makes a dramatic setting for outdoor jazz at the annual Barbados Jazz Festival in January. The park trail leads to a picnic spot overlooking the Scotland District and Atlantic coastline where you might hear the rustle of green monkeys in the treetops above.

🚩 120 C3 ✉ St Peter ☎ 422 3555 🕐 Daily 8:30–6 ✋ Inexpensive
🍴 Café ($) at Barbados Wildlife Reserve opposite 🚌 From Bridgetown, Speightstown and Bathsheba

FAIRMONT ROYAL PAVILION ESTATE

The west coast has many pseudonyms, "Platinum Coast," "Gold Coast" and even "Millionaires' Row", maybe because its sands are silvery or gold, and the hotels ultra-glamorous and extremely expensive. Commanding an historic estate is the Fairmont Royal Pavilion, where writers meet their publishers and where Sir Edward Cunard, one of the world's greatest shipping magnates, lived. Renowned South American-born landscape architect Fernando Tabora created the tropical gardens here. There is a weekly guided botanic tour of the courtyards, beds and lily ponds on Wednesdays at 10am. You follow the head gardener through more than 400 coconut trees. If you're stylishly dressed, you can take afternoon tea in the Café Taboras of the Royal Pavilion. In traditional 1930s manner, a white pot of Earl Grey, Darjeeling, peppermint or camomile tea is brought to your table, accompanied by a tiered stand of chocolate brownies, pastries, jam turnovers and crustless cucumber sandwiches.

✚ 120 E2 ✉ Porters, St James ☎ 422 5555 ⓣ Tour at 10am Wed
🍴 Afternoon tea daily 3:30–5 🚌 From Bridgetown or Speightstown

FOLKESTONE MARINE RESERVE

Not solely of interest to scuba divers, the park tells the story of the marine life of the island through its museum. Here you'll learn interesting snippets: for example, did you know the sex of a sea turtle is

determined by the temperature of the sand the eggs are laid in? Then rent some equipment and go snorkeling in the sea to see fish, sponges and coral. Nearby, glass-bottomed boat tours will take you out to Dottins Reef wrecks and the reefs.

🚑 120 F2 ✉ Folkestone, St James ☎ 422 2314 🕐 Park open daily, museum Mon–Fri 9–5 ✋ Park free, museum inexpensive 🍴 Beach bars, cafés and a picnic area 🚌 From Speightstown, Holetown and Bridgetown

FRANK HUTSON SUGAR MUSEUM

Yet another property run by the Barbados National Trust is the Sir Frank Hutson Sugar Museum. Its collection of old sugar objects and machinery tells the story of what was once the most prized commodity on the island. The collection was started by Barbadian engineer Sir Frank Hutson and is a tribute to his passion. During the cane-grinding season, from February to May, you can step over to the boiling house at the Portvale Sugar Factory, one of a few factories still working on the island, for a dollop of molasses.

🖰 120 F3 ✉ St James ☎ 426 2421 🕔 Mon–Sat 9–5 (except public hols) ✋ Museum inexpensive, factory tour extra 🍴 Excellent cafés ($–$$) on the coast road 🚌 From Bridgetown take the Rock Hall bus

GRENADE HALL FOREST AND SIGNAL STATION

This is a good place to escape the relentless Caribbean sun. A trail descends through a web of vines and winds on for nearly a mile on paved paths smothered in moss. It's slippery, so wear strong soles with treads. At intervals you'll see questions (forming part of a quiz), plus quotes and anecdotes from the likes of Charles Darwin and an Amerindian chief. These remind us that humans continue to exploit the rainforests of the world for timber. There is a cave that sheltered Arawak Indians and, later, Rastafarians and escaped convicts. Shell tools found here are on display at the Barbados Wildlife Reserve (► 36).

Next door to the forest is the restored, whitewashed tower of the Grenade Hall Signal Station, built in 1819. Barbados had a string of such stations, established following the slave rebellion of 1816. During the uprising, one-fifth of the island's sugar cane fields was set on fire and scores of slaves were killed, executed or deported. The news of the revolt took hours to reach the authorities in Bridgetown, so the following year the governor proposed that a chain of signal stations be built to aid communication. The network relayed messages by flags, to which watchful messengers responded by dispatching the news to headquarters in

Bridgetown. Following the abolition of slavery, the signal stations' crews passed the time by monitoring approaching cargo ships and announcing school times. An audio tape plays as you browse through displays of clay pipe fragments and musket balls. Climb the polished wooden staircase to the lookout at the top and imagine life before the telephone.

✚ 120 C3 ✉ Farley Hill, St Peter ☎ 422 8826 🕐 Daily 10–5, last entry 3:30–3:45 (arrive before 3 to see the monkeys) ✋ Moderate; includes Forest and Signal Station 🚌 From Speightstown

a drive to the island's northern tip

This drive covers the northern tip of the island, from the
parish of St Peter up to St Lucy.

*Head north on the coastal road out of Speightstown,
keeping the sea to your left. Pass the entrance to
Almond Beach Village and Port St Charles Marina and
turn right up a hill. Continue over the junction
(intersection) and look out for All Saints Church.*

Flanked by sugar cane fields, All Saints Church, built in
1649, is the resting place of William Arnold, the first
English settler. His grave is clearly marked.

*Continue to a T-junction (intersection), turn right and
follow signs to the Barbados Wildlife Reserve (➤ 36).*

Farley Hill National Park (▶ 79) appears first, to your left. Park inside and walk around the ruins. Leave the car where it is and cross the road to the Barbados Wildlife Reserve. After seeing the animals, birds and reptiles, have a drink or snack in the café before exploring nearby Grenade Hall Forest and Signal Station (▶ 84).

Leave Farley Hill and follow signs to the Morgan Lewis Sugar Mill (▶ 90 and Cherry Tree Hill. Stop by St Nicholas Abbey, the island's oldest house. You can then loop back to the main road into St Lucy and onto the Animal Flower Cave (▶ 74) and North Point.

At stunning North Point take tea and photos until it's time to head back on the coastal road to Speightstown.

Distance Approx 16 miles (26km)
Time Half a day with lunch, to a full day
Start/End Point Speightstown ✚ 120 D2
Lunch Barbados Wildlife Reserve ($)
❓ If you plan to walk the forest nature trail, wear sturdy shoes and be careful on the mossy paths

HARRISON'S CAVE

Best places to see ➤ 46–47.

HOLETOWN

You can spend a full day in Holetown or, during February, a full week at the annual Holetown Festival. The festival coincides with the landing of the first British settlers to the island on February 17, 1627. Prior to this, English Captain John Powell, sailing the *Olive Blossom* to Brazil, anchored off the small natural harbor and set foot at what he declared Jamestown. Later, the settlement was renamed "the Hole" after a tiny inlet where boats could harbor. Back in England, Powell reported his discovery to his employer, Sir William Courteen, an Anglo-Dutch merchant. Courteen responded by sending out an expedition of about 80 settlers and a group of African slaves captured from a Spanish galleon. Powell headed the mission, sailing the

William and John. More white settlers followed, setting up home and establishing crops of cotton, ginger and tobacco. They soon found out how to tend and utilize the soil using methods taught to them by Arawak Indians brought over especially from Guyana. Commemorating the landing is the Holetown Monument on the forecourt of the town's police station, the former fort. The date, for some reason, mistakenly reads 1605.

Around the town are a few buildings dating from the 17th century. St James was the first church, originally built of wood. Inside is the old font and a bell inscribed "God Bless King William, 1696." Modern gems include the exceptional Patisserie Flindt, plus a chattel village of craft shops and an art gallery.

➕ 120 F2 ✉ St James 🍴 Excellent cafés and bars ($–$$) 🚌 From Bridgetown, Speightstown and Bathsheba

MORGAN LEWIS SUGAR MILL

At one time Barbados had many wind-driven mills. They were introduced by the Dutch planters from Brazil when they brought sugar cane to the island in the 1600s, flattening the forests to make way for vast plantations worked by slaves from Africa. The mills crushed the sugar cane to extract the juice, which would then go through a process of boiling and cooling before finally ending up as sugar for export.

Built around 1776, the restored Morgan Lewis Sugar Mill is the largest complete windmill in the Caribbean. It is set within a working farm and occupies a gorgeous location, flanked by a row of mahogany trees. Inside is the grinding machinery, made by a firm in Derby, England. Although not as vital as tourism, the sugar industry is still important to Barbados.

✚ 120 C4 ✉ Near Cherry Tree Hill, St Andrew ☎ 422 7429 ⏰ Mon–Sat 9–5 💰 Moderate

ST NICHOLAS ABBEY

Just beyond the magnificent lookout of Cherry Tree Hill in St Andrew, St Nicholas Abbey is a wonderful, Jacobean-style plantation house, believed to be one of only three still standing in the western hemisphere and recently beautifully renovated. The house was built in 1650 and is supposedly the oldest in Barbados, although it was never an abbey. During the days of slavery, it was a working sugar plantation. Its past is riddled with scandal; the original owner, Colonel Benjamin Berringer, was killed in a duel with his neighbor, John Yeamans, after Yeamans had an affair with Berringer's wife. Yeamans then married the wife but the two fled the island in 1669 for Carolina, unable to cope with the prejudices of the day, and Yeamans became governor of the colony after only three years.

Guided tours of the ground floor take place, to see the cedar paneling, Dutch gables and Chinese Chippendale staircase.

www.stnicholasabbey.com

🔁 120 C4 ✉ Cherry Tree Hill, St Peter ☎ 422 8725 🕐 Daily 10–3:30

✋ Inexpensive

SIX MEN'S BAY

At the coastal village of Six Men's Bay wooden fishing boats, waiting to be treated or repaired, are pulled up onto the grass beyond the shoreline. Nets and floats lie scattered about, as do chunks of mahogany used by boatbuilders to make the keels. If you're lucky, you might see work being carried out. Usually the boatbuilders don't mind if you stop to chat or ask questions. Pretty wooden houses line one side of the road while the sea laps the sands opposite, making this a refreshing place to rest before reaching Speightstown.

🔁 120 C2 ✉ Near Speightstown

🍴 Rum shops and restaurants in Speightstown ($–$$) 🚌 Speightstown bus from Bridgetown

SPEIGHTSTOWN
Best places to see ➤ 50–51.

WELCHMAN HALL GULLY
Formed by a series of caves that collapsed, the gully is a 0.62-mile (1km) corridor of tropical jungle cutting through the coral foundations of the island. Cliffs rise up on either side, and banana, nutmeg and fig trees are among the 200 or so species of tropical plant that grow in the gully. It is said to take its name from a Welsh settler called Williams who once owned the land through which the ravine cuts. His descendants planted some of the trees.

The National Trust, which takes care of the site, has added a few plants but it's pretty much left in a wild state. As you walk through, it is easy to imagine how Barbados must have looked before the first settlers arrived and carried out a program of ravaging deforestation. At one end a stalactite and stalagmite have met in the middle to form a 46-in (118-cm) diameter column that appears to be holding up the cliff. If you're present around dawn or dusk, you might spot Barbados green monkeys.

✚ 120 F4 ✉ St Thomas ☎ 438 6671 ⏰ Daily 9–5 (except public hols)
✋ Moderate 🚌 From Bridgetown take the Sturges bus ❓ Wear good walking shoes and take drinking water

a walk along the Arbib Nature and Heritage Trail

The Arbib Nature and Heritage Trail – run by the Barbados National Trust – won the Caribbean ecotourism award, beating entrants from 20 other islands. There are two trails of varying length: the longer "Whim Adventure" trail cuts through the Whim Gully, one of many ravines of limestone and coral that lead to the sea and drain the island's rainfall. Get the most from the trail by taking a guided walk.

The trail begins from Speightstown (although it isn't well marked) and passes villages, sugar cane plantations and cottonfields. As you go, the guide stops to point out herbs and other plants that have medicinal uses, such

as the castor-oil plant. You will weave through mango, banana and grapefruit trees, dog's dumpling, breadfruit, the bearded fig and a pumpkin patch.

In the interior villages you'll see Barbadian chattel houses (the traditional homes of plantation workers), some with their own kitchen gardens. The chattel is built perfectly symmetrically with a door in the center and windows either side. Traditionally the roof is made of shingle, with a steep pitch to allow rain to run off easily. Surprisingly, these tiny buildings withstand hurricanes pretty well, too.

As the walk nears the coast the houses become grander. You can rest near the cannon at the remains of 18th-century Dover Fort, overlooking the water-front apartments of Port St Charles, before heading to Speightstown. Stroll back along the sandy beach in front of the Almond Beach Village before joining your guide for a drink at the rum shop at Speightstown harborside.

Distance 5 miles (8km); alternative
3.5 miles (5.5km) trail
Time 2 or 3.5 hours, depending on stops
Start/End Point Speightstown 120 D2
Lunch Various places in Speightstown ($–$$)
Walks operate Wed, Thu, Sat at 9:30 and 2:30 and must be reserved. Wear proper walking shoes, a sun hat, sunscreen and take drinking water (426 2421)

Southern Barbados

In the south of Barbados you will find the bustling capital, Bridgetown, and the airport, with attractions coming thick and fast between the two, all within easy reach of one another. Inland, however, forested terrain slopes upward to Gun Hill, from which there are amazing views right across the island.

Oistins

On the coast, dramatic cliffs rise up past South Point Lighthouse, sandy beaches and big rollers at their base, attracting surfers. The island's party scene is along the southwest coast at St Lawrence Gap, a fun-packed strip of bars, clubs, craft stalls, rum shacks and less expensive hotels, ideal for a family vacation.

BANKS (BARBADOS) BREWERIES

Wherever you go on the island you'll see black, red and white billboards announcing that, apart from rum, the only thing to drink on Barbados is Banks beer. During a tour of the brewery and "Brew-seum", just outside Bridgetown, you can see it being brewed, visit the old brew house and have a tasting. Notice that the copper kettles, used for the brewing process for 30 years, have been replaced by modern steel vats that can each hold 3,080gal (14,000L) of beer. Even more astounding is the bottling hall, where 250,000 bottles of Banks are capped each day.

🕂 124 E1 ⊠ St Michael ☎ 228 6846 🕓 Tours: Mon–Fri 10, 12 and 2. Closed Wed 👖 Inexpensive 🍴 Bar for beer tasting, cafés and restaurants ($–$$$) in Bridgetown 🚌 From Bridgetown

BARBADOS CONCORDE EXPERIENCE

A brand new attraction situated at Grantley Adams International Airport, giving visitors a chance to find out all they ever wanted to know about Concorde, which used to fly regularly to the island.

There's an interactive flight school, a departure lounge, an observation deck, and a multimedia interactive presentation projected along the entire length of the aircraft and including live sound effects of Concorde taking off and breaking the sound barrier. Visitors can see the cockpit and a simulator, view historic photos of the aircraft and buy memorabilia in the gift shop.

🕂 125 E5 ⊠ Grantley Adams International Airport, Christ Church 🕓 Daily 9–6 👖 Moderate

THE CRANE

Try to visit this historic hotel on a Sunday morning so you can enjoy the brunch and foot-tapping live gospel by local singers. It takes place in the clifftop terrace restaurant overlooking the cliffs and the Atlantic. On one side is the hotel pool: the majestic white colonnades surrounding a circle of blue and backed by the ocean have been photographed by dozens of fashion magazines. On the other side, sheer cliffs drop to the pink sands of Crane Beach.

Opened in 1887 on the site of an 18th-century mansion and lit

by oil lamps, The Crane was the first resort hotel on Barbados. At that time, ladies bathed discreetly in a specially built area called "the horse". The original steps cut into the cliff, leading to "the horse", still remain. As for the name of the hotel, it came about when there was a small commercial port here and a crane was used to raise and lower cargo on and off the trading ships that docked.

✚ 125 D6 ✉ Crane, St Philip ☎ 423 6220 ⏱ Brunch Sun 9:30am; singing Sun 10–11am; Bajan buffet Sun 12:30–3. Advance reservations essential ❚❙ Restaurant ($$–$$$) noted for its seafood, especially oysters ▣ From Bridgetown catch the Sam Lord bus

GRAEME HALL BIRD SANCTUARY

Just down the road from the lively St Lawrence Gap is an unlikely setting for a bird sanctuary, but this beautiful mangrove swamp is an oasis of calm in comparison to the coastal strip. The Graeme Hall Swamp is the island's largest expanse of inland water, home to two types of mangrove and 40 species of bird from sandpipers to cattle egrets. Follow the boardwalks around the swamp and look for green monkeys, mongoose and in the water below, tarpon

fish. There is an enclosed area where you can admire the scarlet ibis, parrots and flamingos. Information boards tell you about the trees and there's a migratory bird exhibit. It's a great afternoon out for families, painters, photographers, birdwatchers or anybody looking for a tranquil place simply to sit and contemplate the scenery.

www.graemehall.com

✚ 124 E1 ✉ Worthing ☎ 435 9727 ⏰ Daily 8–6 🍴 Café and shop ($)

GUN HILL SIGNAL STATION

Even if you've already visited Grenade Hall Signal Station (➤ 84) and learned about the signal stations' important role in the early communications network of Barbados, Gun Hill Signal Station is still worth a visit for the views. It was built in 1818 and was reputedly the cream of the string of stations established to warn of slave uprisings. Eventually they served as lookouts for cargo ships. Restored by the Barbados National Trust in 1982, Gun Hill, perched on a ridge overlooking the St George Valley and the south of the island, features a gray flag tower. For travelers with time it's a quiet place to while away a few hours or wait for the best views, which occur around sunset. Look for the British Military Lion, a white figure carved from limestone in the 19th century by the adjutant-general of the Imperial Forces, who was stationed on the island. A plaque below the lion states his name and reads that the British lion shall "…rule from the sea to the ends of the earth."

✚ 124 C2 ✉ St George ☎ 429 1358 ⊕ Mon–Sat 9–5 🍴 Café ($); opening hours restricted 🚌 From Bridgetown take the Sergeant Street bus

HERITAGE PARK AND FOURSQUARE RUM DISTILLERY

Voted by a newspaper in the United States as "one of the most modern rum distilleries in the world," the Heritage Park and Foursquare Rum Distillery comes complete with its own integrated recycling plant. If that alone isn't a sufficient draw, there is plenty more to see at this attraction, which covers 7 acres (3ha) of a once sprawling sugar plantation and includes one of the island's oldest sugar factories. In an outdoor museum filled with machinery, you can see how rum was made in the early days, or you can go underground to the furnace and feel what it was like to be a boiler worker. Nowadays, the distillery is known for its top-selling ESAF White Rum, Orland Brigand and Doorly's Rum, which, naturally, you are given the opportunity to taste.

Capitalizing on the popularity of the Heritage Park, there are exhibitions of paintings by local artists in the on-site art galleries. There are also demonstrations of glass blowing and screen printing, and regular lunch and dinner cultural shows in the Cane Pit Amphitheatre.

✚ 125 D5 ✉ Foursquare, St Philip ☎ 420 1977 🕐 Mon–Fri 9–5 ✋ Moderate; includes access to the beach 🍴 Sugar Cane Café ($–$$) 🚌 From Bridgetown take the St Patrick bus ❓ 40-minute tour available for cruise parties only who book in advance

OCEAN PARK AQUARIUM

Ocean Park is a relatively new project, with 26 displays of marine life from the Caribbean and beyond. Great care has been taken to create natural settings, including fresh water pools and piranha tanks set into rocks, a stand of mangrove trees and a living reef, under which a perspex tunnel has been set. There's a big tank containing nurse and blacktip reef sharks, which are fed every day, and an open-air touch pool where children can handle starfish and conches. In addition, there's an adventure playground, mini golf, a gift shop and a small café serving fantastic fruit smoothies.
www.oceanparkbarbados.com

🚩 124 E3 ⊠ Balls, Christ Church ☎ 420 7405 ③ Summer Tue–Sun 10–6; winter daily 10–5 🖐 Moderate 🍴 Café ($–$$)

OISTINS

Oistins is a busy fishing village that supplies fresh fish and shellfish to the whole of the island. Boats are forever landing catches or are pulled up on the sand dunes for repair or paintwork. Walk among the lobster pots and nets, then watch the fishmongers gutting and packing the fish at the fish terminal. You can get a cheap bite to eat at lunchtime, but the real draw is the popular Friday night Fish Fry, when stallholders fry flying fish, dolphin, shark, barracuda and snapper. Order your fish with rice or a helping of macaroni cheese pie and a bottle of Banks beer. There's music, long lines at the counters and dancing by the tables. Saturday nights are also popular, but even better is the Oistins Fish Festival, which runs over Easter.

🚩 124 F3 ⊠ Christ Church 🍴 Excellent freshly fried fish at stalls ($) 🚌 From Bridgetown

ORCHID WORLD

Best places to see ➤ 42–43.

RAGGED POINT

An old lighthouse marks Ragged Point, the most easterly point of the island. It is a wonderfully exposed, tranquil spot. Though the lighthouse is no longer open to the public, its beams still warn ships away from the limestone cliffs and Cobbler's Reef. Slightly to the north of the lighthouse is tiny, uninhabited Culpepper Island, Barbados's only "colony".

✚ 125 B7 ✉ St Philip 🍴 Cafés and restaurants ($–$$$) en route 🚌 To Crane Beach or Sam Lord's Castle 🎟 Free

ST GEORGE VALLEY

St George Valley is an agricultural oasis covered with sugar cane fields. St George Parish Church stands proudly as one of only four churches on the island to survive the hurricane of 1831. Built in 1784, the church boasts a splendid altar painting called *Rise to Power*. It is the work of artist Benjamin West, the first American president of the Royal Academy. And remember the statue of Lord Nelson in Bridgetown? Well, the sculptor, Richard Westmacott, also created some sculptures here inside the church.

✚ 124 C2

a drive and Sunday brunch

One Sunday morning, having reserved tickets in advance, skip breakfast and head along the south coast to hear gospel singing at The Crane hotel (► 99). En route you'll see Bajan women in dresses, hats and white gloves attending church. Some men wear their Sunday best suits. Quietly and unobtrusively, stop outside any church and listen to the hymns.

Start from Oistins (► 105) on the Maxwell main road and head east, following the signs to the airport. You'll drive through villages with painted houses and cane fields. Follow the signs to Crane Beach.

Arrive at The Crane hotel at 9:30am in time for Sunday brunch at 10:30 and enjoy the entertainment (advance reservations are essential). Afterward, walk down to Crane Bay for swimming, sunbathing or body boarding.

Drive out of Crane Beach and head north finishing up at Ragged Point (► 106) for a brief walk and lunch (if you're still hungry).

On the drive back you can take a right detour to Sunbury Plantation House (► 52) for afternoon tea before heading back towards Oistins.

If the day is still young, take a left detour through small communities to reach Silver Sands beach (► 111).

Watch the windsurfers flip 360 degrees above the waves. Look for the South Point Lighthouse, made in England out of cast iron and shipped in pieces to the island. It was reassembled and working by 1852.

Alternatively, head back along the coastal road to Oistins fishing village for the perfect finale – a succulent fish fry in the open air at one of the many shacks.

Distance Approx 7 miles (12km)
Time Half a day with brunch and stops
Start Point Oistins ✚ 124 F3 **End Point** Ragged Point ✚ 125 B7
Brunch The Crane hotel ($$–$$$) (▶ 99)

ST LAWRENCE GAP

Moving westward along the south coast, the closer you get to Bridgetown the livelier it becomes. St Lawrence Gap is where the party people go, although regulars say it's not as friendly and easy-going as it used to be. Sports bars with video screens, live blues, happy hours and karaoke, souvenir shells and painted maracas are what it's all about. There's a string of good restaurants and, in between the hotels and apartment buildings, crescents of sandy beach and safe swimming. You can learn to dive, water-ski or just hang on to a banana boat.

🚩 124 E1 ✉ South coast, east of Bridgetown 🍴 Bars and restaurants ($–$$), some with live music 🚌 Any south coast bus from Bridgetown

SILVER SANDS

Silver Sands beach at the southern tip of the island is a Mecca for professional windsurfers, and there's a Club Mistral center here for lessons and equipment rental. In addition to windsurfing you can try boogie boarding, hiking and wilderness and adventure diving. As the beach's name suggests less adventurous types can relax on the beautiful silver sands and watch others hard at play.

✚ 124 F3 ⊠ Silver Sands, Christ Church 🍴 Snacks ($) nearby

SUNBURY PLANTATION HOUSE

Best places to see ➤ 52–53.

WILDEY HOUSE

Wildey House, a Georgian hilltop mansion set in beautiful grounds, is the headquarters of the Barbados National Trust. Although the building is not in the best state of repair, visitors will see historic photographs of Barbados and exquisite silver displayed among antique furniture in carefully decorated rooms. The Trust is important to the island because it enables its architecture,

sometimes dating back more than 350 years, to be preserved and maintained. Since 1961 the Trust has taken on the care of eight properties, including a wooded gully (➤ 92), the largest sugar mill in the Caribbean (➤ 83) and a botanic garden (➤ 34). It has also helped to create an underwater park on the west coast and has identified the house on Bush Hill (George Washington House ➤ 68) as the house in which George Washington, president of the United States, stayed in 1751.

✠ 124 D1 ✉ Wildey, St Michael ☎ 426 2421 ◷ By appointment

A submarine cruise

There are few places in the world where you can board a real submarine and submerge for an undersea exploration. Complete with Captain Nemo-style sounds and live dialogue between the crew and the surface, the Atlantis Submarine trip is pricey, but shouldn't be missed.

First, you board the *Ocean Crest* catamaran and sail out of Bridgetown's harbor to reach the submarine. Safety instructions are given before you are invited to board.

In 1994 *Atlantis* became the world's first passenger submarine. Stretching 66ft (20m) and displacing 80 tons, the *Atlantis III* sinks slowly to 151ft (46m). It then cruises gently above the seabed off the west coast at 1.5 knots. You sit with the other passengers on benches, facing outward through large portholes.

The seabed is white, like fallen snow. A wreck appears, the fish darting in and out of its gaps. Next comes a garden of brain coral, ferns and sponges. If you're lucky, a turtle might glide gracefully by. You'll definitely see thousands of fish, from stingrays to barracudas and shoals of colorful species. If you've ever wanted to scuba dive but lacked the courage, this is the next best thing.

Even more spectacular is Atlantis By Night, a cruise taken when the coral is at its most striking and nocturnal predators come out to feed. The submarine's lights

illuminate the coral and fish and you'll see the wreck of the *Lord Willoughby*. Whichever trip you take, at the end you're given a certificate to prove that you took the plunge.

Time 1 hour
Start/End point Atlantis Submarines ✉ Shallow Draught, Bridgetown ☎ 436 8929; www.atlantisadventures.com
🖐 Expensive 🚌 Nearest bus station is Bridgetown; take a taxi to the harbor ❓ Book through Atlantis Submarines, a tour operator, or your hotel or resort rep. **Lunch** Sublime Café ($)

Index

Acknowledgements

The Automobile Association would like to thank the following photographers and companies for their assistance in the preparation of this book. Abbreviations for the picture credits are as follows – (t) top; (b) bottom; (c) centre; (l) left; (r) right; (AA) AA World Travel Library.

4l Near Heroes Square, Bridgetown, AA/J Tims; **4c** Bathsheba, AA/J Tims; **4r** St Lawrence, AA/J Tims; **5l** Mullins Bay, AA/J Tims; **5c** Fairmont Royal Pavilion Hotel, AA/J Tims; **6** Farley Hill Mansion, AA/J Tims; **7** Conch shell, AA/J Tims; **8-9** Animal Flower Cave, AA/J Tims; **10-11** Paynes Bay, AA/J Tims; **12** Bottom Bay, AA/J Tims; **13** Fortitude, Montefiore Fountain, AA/J Tims; **14** Andromeda Botanic Gardens, AA/J Tims; **15** Independence Arch, Bridgetown, AA/J Tims; **16-17** Gibbes Bay, AA/J Tims; **18-19** Near Heroes Square, Bridgetown, AA/J Tims; **22** Holetown Dooflicky Festival, AA/J Tims; **23** Cruise ship, AA/D Lyons; **24** Helicopter, AA/L K Stow; **25** Bathsheba, AA/J Tims; **26** Taxi rank, AA/J Tims; **27** Telephone box, AA/J Tims; **28** Policeman, AA/J Tims; **30** Viewpoint, Scotland District, AA/P Baker; **32-33** Bathsheba, AA/J Tims; **34cl** Hibiscus flower, Andromeda Botanic Gardens, AA/J Tims; **34cb** Hibiscus Cafe, Andromeda Botanic Gardens, AA/J Tims; **34-35** Andromeda Botanic Gardens, AA/J Tims; **35tr** Talipot Palm trees, Corypha umbraculifera, Andromeda Botanic Gardens, AA/J Tims; **36c** Barbados Green or Vervet monkey, Barbados Wildlife Reserve, AA/J Tims; **36bl** Iguanas, Barbados Wildlife Reserve, AA/J Tims; **37t** Barbados Wildlife Reserve, AA/J Tims; **37c** Goose, Barbados Wildlife Reserve, AA/J Tims; **38c** Surfing, Bathsheba, AA/J Tims; **38-39b** Bathsheba, AA/J Tims; **39t** Shop, Bathsheba, AA/J Tims; **40** Highland Pottery, AA/J Tims; **41t** View from the Highland Pottery, AA/J Tims; **41cr** Vase for sale, Highland Pottery, AA/J Tims; **41br** Bar, Chalky Mount Village, AA/J Tims; **42l** Red Ginger Flower, Alpinia purpurata, Flower Forest, AA/J Tims; **42-43c** Palms, Flower Forest, AA/J Tims; **43r** Flower detail, Flower Forest, AA/J Tims; **44l** Clock tower and Cannon, Main Guard, Garrison Historic Area, AA/J Tims; **44/45c** St Ann's Fort, Garrison Historic Area, AA/J Tims; **45t** Race Day, Garrison Savannah, AA/J Tims; **46-47** Harrison's Cave, Tony Arruza/CORBIS; **48b** National Heroes Square, Bridgetown, AA/J Tims; **49tr** Nelson's Monument, National Heroes Square, Bridgetown, AA/J Tims; **49cr** War Memorial, Heroes Square, Bridgetown, AA/J Tims; **50b** Pier, Speightstown, AA/J Tims; **50-51t** Speightstown, AA/J Tims; **51c** St Peter's Church, Speightstown, AA/J Tims; **52t** Prints of paintings by Augustino Brunias (1771), Sunbury Plantation House, AA/J Tims; **52cl** Desk, Sunbury Plantation House, AA/J Tims; **52cr** Marble hip bath, circa 1874, Sunbury Plantation House, AA/J Tims; **53b** Sunbury Plantation House, AA/J Tims; **54-55** Boardwalk, St Lawrence, AA/J Tims; **57** War memorial, Heroes Square, Bridgetown, AA/J Tims; **58tl** Jewish Synagogue, Bridgetown, AA/J Tims; **58/59c** The Careenage, Bridgetown, AA/J Tims; **59br** The Careenage, Bridgetown, AA/J Tims; **60** Montefiore Fountain, Bridgetown, AA/J Tims; **61t** Detail, Parliament buildings, Bridgetown, AA/J Tims; **61b** Parliament buildings, Bridgetown, AA/J Tims; **62-63t** St Michael's Cathedral, Bridgetown, AA/J Tims; **63b** Bridgetown, AA/J Tims; **64-65t** Queen's Park, Bridgetown, AA/J Tims; **64bl** Bandstand, Queen's Park, Bridgetown, AA/J Tims; **65tr** St Michael's Cathedral, Bridgetown, AA/J Tims; **65b** St Michael's Cathedral, Bridgetown, AA/J Tims; **66** Barbados Museum, Bridgetown, AA/J Tims; **69t** Work by Indigenous Potteries, Pelican Craft Village, Bridgetown Indigenous Potteries/AA/J Tims; **69b** Pelican Craft Village, Bridgetown, AA/J Tims; **70b** Pottery, Chattel House Settlement, Tyrol Cot Heritage Village, AA/J Tims; **71** Chattel House Settlement, Tyrol Cot Heritage Village, AA/J Tims; **72** Bathsheba, AA/J Tims; **73** Farley Hill mansion, AA/J Tims; **74t** Animal Flower Cave, AA/J Tims; **74b** North Point, Animal Flower Cave, AA/J Tims; **75t** Barbados Polo Club, AA/J Tims; **77t** Bathsheba, AA/J Tims; **77b** Round House Bar, Cattlewash, AA/J Tims; **78bl** Earthworks Pottery, AA/J Tims; **78br** Earthworks Pottery, AA/J Tims; **79t** Farley Hill mansion, AA/J Tims; **80t** Fairmount Royal Pavilion Hotel, AA/J Tims; **81** Fairmount Royal Pavilion Hotel, AA/J Tims; **82-83t** Beach, Folkestone Marine Park and Museum, AA/J Tims; **82b** Folkestone Marine Park and Museum, AA/J Tims; **83b** Frank Hutson Sugar Museum, AA/J Tims; **84tl** Grenade Hall Forest and Signal Station, AA/J Tims; **85b** Grenade Hall Forest Signal Station, AA/J Tims; **86** Farley Hill National Park, AA/J Tims; **87** Animal Flower Cave, AA/J Tims; **88-89t** Holetown Chattel building, AA/J Tims; **88bl** Holetown Festival, AA/J Tims; **90tl** Morgan Lewis Windmill, AA/P Baker; **90-91c** Six Men's Bay, AA/J Tims; **91r** Six Men's Bay, AA/J Tims; **92-93** Welchman Hall Tropical Park, AA/J Tims; **94** Harbour Promenade, Speightstown, AA/J Tims; **95** Arbib Nature and Heritage Trail, AA/L K Stow; **96** Dover beach, St Lawrence, AA/J Tims; **97** Restaurants, St Lawrence, AA/J Tims; **98t** Banks Brewery, AA/J Tims; **98-99c** Crane Beach Hotel, AA/J Tims; **99b** Crane Beach from Crane Beach Hotel, AA/J Tims; **100-101** Egret Island, Graeme Hall Nature Reserve, AA/J Tims; **102** View from Gun Hill Signal Station, AA/J Tims; **103t** Foursquare Rum Distillery, AA/J Tims; **104** Harbour, Oistins, AA/J Tims; **105** Oistin's Friday night Fish Fry, AA/J Tims; **106** Ragged Point lighthouse, AA/J Tims; **107** Sugar cane, St George Valley, AA/J Tims; **108l** Oistin's fish market, AA/J Tims; **109t** Ragged Point, AA/J Tims; **109b** Crane beach, AA/J Tims; **110-111b** St Lawrence, AA/J Tims; **111t** Dover beach, St Lawrence, AA/J Tims; **112-113b** Wildey House, AA/J Tims; **113t** Reading room, Wildey House, AA/J Tims; **114-115** Atlantis Submarine, AA/L K Stow.

Every effort has been made to trace the copyright holders, and we apologise in advance for any accidental errors. We would be happy to apply the corrections in the following edition of this publication.

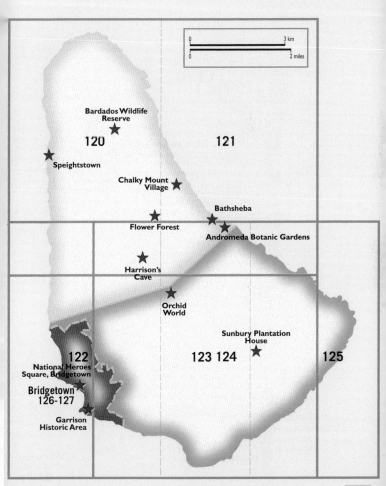

★ Best places to see   ■ Featured sight

Bridgetown and Around

Southern Barbados

Northern Barbados

0 _____ 3 km
0 _____ 2 miles

★ Bardados Wildlife Reserve

120   121

★ Speightstown

★ Chalky Mount Village

Bathsheba

★ Flower Forest   ★ Andromeda Botanic Gardens

★ Harrison's Cave

★ Orchid World

Sunbury Plantation House ★

122   123 124   125

National Heroes Square, Bridgetown

Bridgetown 126–127

★ Garrison Historic Area

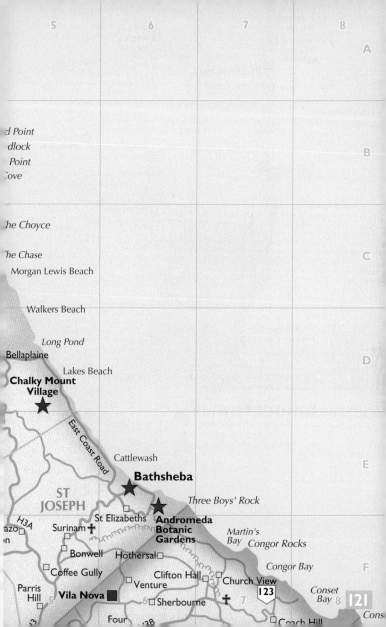

A   5   6   7   8

B
d Point
dlock
Point
ove

C
he Choyce

he Chase
Morgan Lewis Beach

Walkers Beach

Long Pond
Bellaplaine

D
Lakes Beach
Chalky Mount Village
★

East Coast Road

E
Cattlewash
Bathsheba
★
ST JOSEPH
Three Boys' Rock

H3A
St Elizabeths
Andromeda Botanic Gardens
★
azo
Surinam ✝
Martin's Bay
Congor Rocks
n
Bonwell
Hothersal

F
Coffee Gully
Congor Bay
Parris Hill
Clifton Hall
Venture
Church View
123
Vila Nova ■
Conset Bay 8
6
Sherbourne
7
Four
Coach Hill
Cons

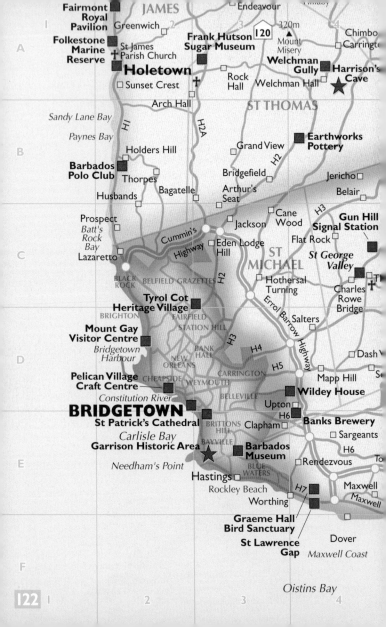

Endeavour

JAMES

Fairmont Royal Pavilion

Greenwich

320m
120
Mount Misery

Chimbo
Carringto

Folkestone Marine Reserve

Frank Hutson Sugar Museum

St James Parish Church

Welchman Gully

Harrison's Cave

Holetown

Rock Hall

Welchman Hall

Sunset Crest

ST THOMAS

Arch Hall

Sandy Lane Bay

H1

H2A

Grand View

Earthworks Pottery

Paynes Bay

Holders Hill

H2

Jericho

Barbados Polo Club

Thorpes

Bridgefield

Belair

Husbands

Bagatelle

Arthur's Seat

Prospect

Cane Wood

H3

Gun Hill Signal Station

Batt's Rock Bay

Jackson

Flat Rock

Cummin's

Eden Lodge

ST MICHAEL

St George Valley

Lazaretto

Highway

Hill

BLACK ROCK

BELFIELD GRAZETTES

H2

Hothersal Turning

Charles Rowe Bridge

T

Tyrol Cot Heritage Village

BRIGHTON

FAIRFIELD

Errol Barrow Highway

Salters

Mount Gay Visitor Centre

STATION HILL

H3

H4

Bridgetown Harbour

BANK HALL

Dash

NEW ORLEANS

CARRINGTON

H5

Pelican Village Craft Centre

CHEAPSIDE

WEYMOUTH

Mapp Hill

Se

Constitution River

BELLEVILLE

Wildey House

BRIDGETOWN

Upton

St Patrick's Cathedral

BRITTONS HILL

H6

Banks Brewery

Clapham

Carlisle Bay

BAYVILLE

Sargeants

Garrison Historic Area

H6

Needham's Point

Barbados Museum

Rendezvous

To

BLUE WATERS

Hastings

Maxwell

Rockley Beach

H7

Maxwell

Worthing

Graeme Hall Bird Sanctuary

Dover

St Lawrence Gap

Maxwell Coast

Oistins Bay

1   2   3   4

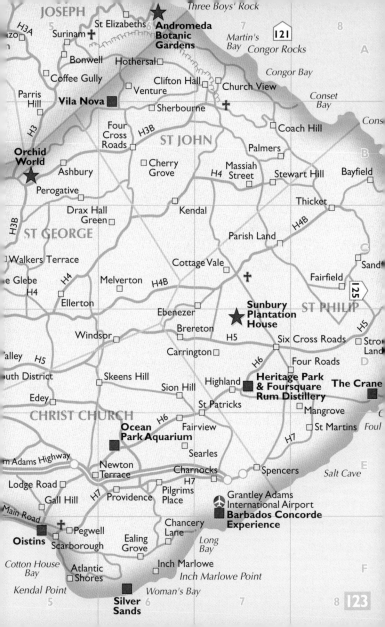

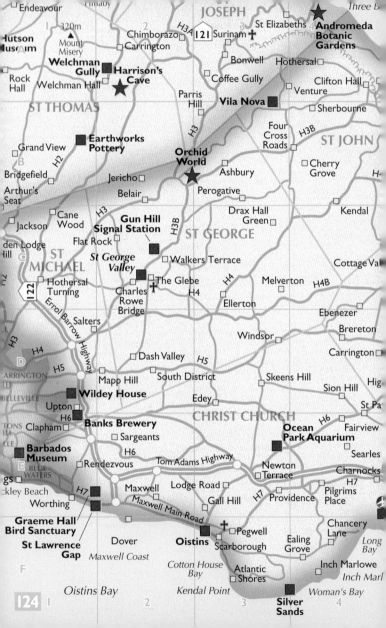

JOSEPH

Endeavour
Finaby
Three b

320m
Mount Misery
Hutson MuseAm
Chimborazo
121
Surinam
St Elizabeths
Andromeda Botanic Gardens

Carrington
Bonwell
Hothersal

Welchman Gully
Harrison's Cave
Coffee Gully
Clifton Hall
Venture

Rock Hall
Welchman Hall
Parris Hill
Vila Nova
Sherbourne

ST THOMAS
Four Cross Roads
ST JOHN

Grand View
Earthworks Pottery
Cherry Grove

Bridgefield
Jericho
Orchid World
Ashbury

Arthur's Seat
Belair
Perogative

Jackson
Cane Wood
Drax Hall Green
Kendal

den Lodge Hill
Gun Hill Signal Station
ST GEORGE

ST MICHAEL
Flat Rock
Walkers Terrace
Cottage Val

Hothersal Turning
122
St George Valley
The Glebe
Melverton

Charles Rowe Bridge
Ellerton
Ebenezer

Errol Barrow Highway
Salters
Windsor
Brereton

Dash Valley
Carrington

ARRINGTON
South District
Skeens Hill
Hig

BELLEVILLE
Wildey House
Mapp Hill
Edey
Sion Hill

Upton
CHRIST CHURCH
St Pa

TONS
Clapham
Banks Brewery
Ocean Park Aquarium
Fairview

Barbados Museum
Sargeants
Newton Terrace
Searles
Charnocks

BLUE WATERS
Rendezvous
Tom Adams Highway
Providence
Pilgrims Place

ckley Beach
Maxwell
Lodge Road
Gall Hill

Worthing
Maxwell Main Road
Chancery Lane

Graeme Hall Bird Sanctuary
Dover
Pegwell
Long Bay

St Lawrence Gap
Maxwell Coast
Oistins
Scarborough
Ealing Grove
Inch Marlowe
Inch Marl

Cotton House Bay
Atlantic Shores

124
Oistins Bay
Kendal Point
Silver Sands
Woman's Bay

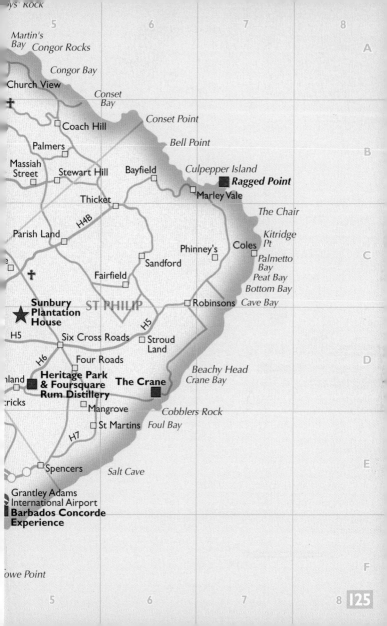

Martin's Bay

Congor Rocks

Congor Bay

Church View ✝

Conset Bay

Coach Hill

Conset Point

Palmers

Bell Point

Massiah Street

Stewart Hill

Bayfield

Culpepper Island

Ragged Point

Thicket

Marley Vale

H4B

The Chair

Parish Land

Phinney's

Coles

Kitridge Pt

Sandford

Palmetto Bay

Fairfield

Peat Bay

Bottom Bay

ST PHILIP

Robinsons

Cave Bay

✝

Sunbury Plantation House

H5

H5

Six Cross Roads

Stroud Land

H6

Four Roads

Beachy Head

Crane Bay

land

Heritage Park & Foursquare Rum Distillery

The Crane

cricks

Mangrove

Cobblers Rock

H7

St Martins

Foul Bay

Spencers

Salt Cave

Grantley Adams International Airport

Barbados Concorde Experience

owe Point

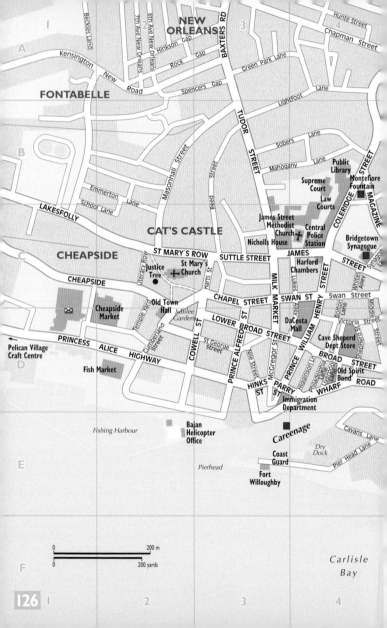

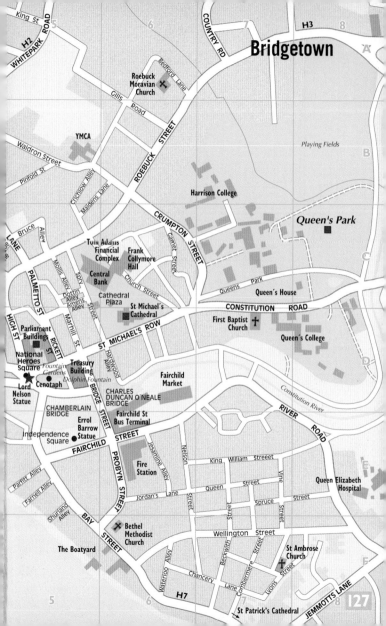

Bridgetown

King St

WHITEPARK ROAD

H2

COUNTRY RD

H3

Bedford Lane

Roebuck Moravian Church

Gills Road

YMCA

Waldron Street

Pinfold St

ROEBUCK STREET

Crichlow Alley

Maidens Lane

Bruce Alley

Playing Fields

Harrison College

Queen's Park

CRUMPTON STREET

Camet Street

Tom Adams Financial Complex

Frank Collymore Hall

LANE

PALMETTO ST

Mollis Alley

Spry St

Dottin Alley

Amens Alley

Marhill St

Central Bank

Church Street

Cathedral Plaza

St Michael's Cathedral

Queens Park

Queen's House

CONSTITUTION ROAD

HIGH ST

RICKET ST

ST MICHAEL'S ROW

First Baptist Church

Queen's College

Parliament Buildings

National Heroes Square

Fountain Gardens

Cenotaph

Treasury Building

Dolphin Fountain

Harwood Alley

Fairchild Market

Constitution River

Lord Nelson Statue

CHAMBERLAIN BRIDGE

BRIDGE STREET

CHARLES DUNCAN O'NEALE BRIDGE

Fairchild St Bus Terminal

RIVER ROAD

Errol Barrow Statue

Independence Square

FAIRCHILD STREET

PROBYN STREET

Fire Station

Jesamine Alley

King William Streeet

Nelson Street

Queen Street

Vine Street

Queen Elizabeth Hospital

Parfitt Alley

Farrell Alley

Jordan's Lane

Spruce Street

Shurland Alley

BAY STREET

Bethel Methodist Church

Wellington Street

Beckwith Street

Combermere Street

St Ambrose Church

Lyons Street

The Boatyard

Waterloo Alley

Chancery Lane

H7

St Patrick's Cathedral

JEMMOTTS LANE

127

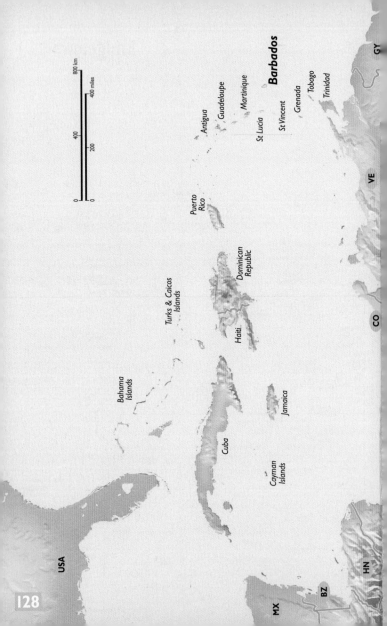

USA

MX

BZ

HN

Bahama Islands

Cayman Islands

Cuba

Jamaica

Turks & Caicos Islands

Haiti

Dominican Republic

Puerto Rico

Antigua

Guadeloupe

Martinique

St Lucia

St Vincent

Barbados

Grenada

Tobago

Trinidad

VE

CO

GY

0   200   400

0   400   800 km

miles